D1092591

1 2 3 4 5 6 7 ← P Y → 9 8 7 6 5 4 3

HUNTING THE DESERT WHALE

William Morrow and Company

New York   1960

Hunting the Desert Whale

Personal Adventures in Baja California by
ERLE STANLEY GARDNER

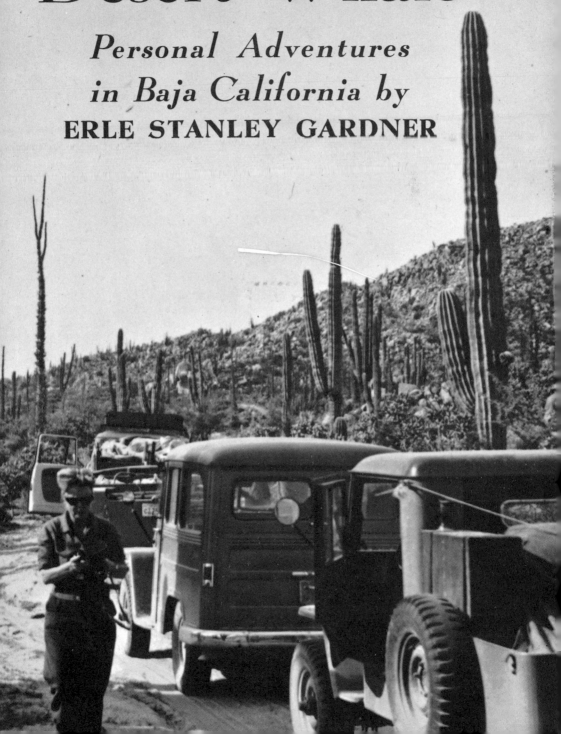

CONTENTS

ILLUSTRATIONS

ILLUSTRATIONS

ILLUSTRATIONS

ILLUSTRATIONS

HUNTING THE DESERT WHALE

United Press International Photo

Taken by the Tiros weather satellite's wide angle camera, this photograph of lower Baja California shows Scammon's Lagoon (see arrow), the annual rendezvous of the desert whale.

ANTICIPATION
AND TEMPTATION

My friend, Murl Emery, is a devastating influence.

To begin with, Emery won't fall in step with the world. He won't buckle down to business in the orthodox sense, and he insists upon living a life of variety and adventure. When he finds himself confronted with the need for money he throws his bedroll and a few provisions into his four-wheel drive pick-up, puts in fifty gallons of gasoline and a like amount of drinking water, drives out into the desert and finds a mine.

Ordinarily, one would say that was a better way to spend money than to make money. But it doesn't work that way with Murl. He finds the mines. He gets his money out of the ground. Sometimes it takes longer than it does other times but he invariably gets what he goes after.

The unorthodox Murl.

Nothing works according to logic or the laws of averages with Murl.

The guy has an encyclopedic knowledge of minerals, a rough-and-ready knowledge of geology, he knows the desert from one end to the other, and he has a supreme contempt for civilization.

For many years now Murl has made his living in this unorthodox fashion. He probably spends more time in camp than he does at home. He is completely self-reliant and thoroughly original, both in thinking and behavior.

Murl Emery was raised on the Colorado River. His father spent his life on the Colorado and Murl's son, Pat, has, for nearly all the thirty years of his life, been on the Colorado.

In Murl's earlier days the Colorado River was very different from what it is now. Living on it was a career in itself. The Colorado was a big, untamed, roaring, dangerous body of water swirling its way through narrow canyons, expanding to a placid stream for a mile or two, then boiling into new rapids. From the time it left the Grand Canyon it flowed through a bleak desert where a man had to know a lot about nature just to survive. Every year the river took its grim toll of human life.

Murl Emery knew the river when it was rough and rugged and he in turn became rough and rugged like the river.

Then civilization entered the picture. The Hoover Dam was constructed and following that, other dams "tamed" the river until it became a succession of lakes. Where formerly only the hard-bitten prospector or expert boatman dared make his way, keen-eyed and wary, now there are paved roads and sportsmen by the thousand come flocking to the new recreation area, carrying boats on trailers, driving cars well stocked with fishing equipment.

The silence of the desert is shattered by the snarl of outboard motors as boats plane along at twenty-five to thirty-five miles an hour or idle along at a leisurely trolling speed.

The development of plastics, of fiberglas, outboard motors, and the construction of dams has changed Murl Emery's environment so it is difficult to recognize—and Murl doesn't like it.

But modern inventions can't change Murl Emery. Environment may change but the man is the same.

What has happened on the Colorado River is only in a small measure what has been happening all over the country. If you question this statement just look at a map today and try to find some reasonably near-by place where there is still adventure; where one must be self-reliant in order to survive.

Strangely enough, however, there is such a place within a few hundred miles of the sprawling population congregated in the congested district of Southern California.

South of San Diego is Tijuana. South of Tijuana is Ensenada. South of Ensenada is adventure unlimited.

Over on the desert side, Calexico is the border city of the Imperial Valley. Through Calexico runs the high fence of the international boundary. South of that fence is Mexicali. A hundred and twenty miles south of Mexicali is the little fishing port of San Felipe. The road is hard surfaced all the way. South of San Felipe there are fifty-three miles of dirt road to the little fishing village of Puertecitos. The trip to Puertecitos can be made by a good driver in an ordinary well-constructed automobile—although it is surprising the number of motorists one will find in trouble on that fifty-three-mile stretch.

South of Puertecitos civilization comes to an abrupt halt. You don't go below Puertecitos unless you have a four-wheel drive automobile, ample stores of gasoline and drinking water, and know what you're doing—that is, you *may* go but you may not come back.

So it was as natural for Murl Emery's attention to gravi-

16

South of Puerticitos civilization comes to an abrupt halt.

tate toward Baja California as it was for an iron filing to gravitate toward a magnet.

As it happened, I had first felt the appeal of Baja California some thirteen years ago, and in 1947 I had engaged in what was in those days a rather spectacular feat: I had driven all the way from California down the twelve hundred miles of "road" to Cabo San Lucas, the end of the peninsula. Then, in 1948, I had repeated the trip.

I had written a book about the 1947 trip, *The Land of Shorter Shadows*—a book which attracted some considerable attention over the years, although it is now out of print.

When Murl Emery became interested in Baja California he had read about everything he could find on the subject. He had therefore read my book and given it a great deal of thought.

Murl's thinking is a combination of three equal parts of desert, water and adventure.

HUNTING THE DESERT WHALE

It was therefore only natural that he should start thinking about the rivers and lagoons in Baja California, and since there aren't any rivers worth mentioning, he naturally started concentrating on the lagoons. And whenever one starts thinking about lagoons in Baja California, Scammon's Lagoon stands out head and shoulders above all the rest.

Every year the gray whales leave the Bering Sea during the winter and start a long, slow journey around the Aleutian Islands, down through the trackless waste of waters, until they reach the coast of California. Then they move along the California Coast, down Baja California, and about the first part of January begin to show up in numbers in Scammon's Lagoon. Here they breed and here in alternate years the cows bear their young.

Because of our mutual interest in Baja California it was inevitable that Emery and I should get together. And it was only natural that Emery should start talking Scammon's Lagoon to me. And when he started talking Scammon's Lagoon, it was only natural that I should listen and that my life should be disrupted.

Scammon's Lagoon stands out head and shoulders above the rest.

In vain I pointed out to Emery that in the last thirteen years my life had undergone a great change. I had speaking commitments all over the country. I was interested in a television show which was on for an hour every week and frequently created big problems.

On my 1948 trip down the peninsula I had been accompanied by Harry Steeger and his wife. Harry Steeger is the owner of Argosy Magazine, and around the campfires we had discussed the problem of innocent men who have wrongfully been convicted of crime. We discussed the better administration of justice; better law enforcement; and from those conversations came the Court of Last Resort.

At that time neither Steeger nor I had any idea of the magnitude of the task we were undertaking; of how this idea of the Court of Last Resort would capture the imagination of the reading public; or the amount of time we were going to be called on to donate in carrying on the work.

In those days my headquarters at Temecula were isolated. I didn't have a telephone on the place and didn't want one. Now I have telephones all over the ranch. My long distance bill is astronomical. My work for the Court of Last Resort and my speaking engagements keep me zigzagging around the country by airplane and automobile. The very idea of breaking away from all this in order to adventure into Baja California was fantastic. I explained all this to Emery.

Emery's only answer was to spread out a map of Baja California and, with the stubby nail of his right index finger, gently tap Scammon's Lagoon.

Finally, despairing of pulling me away from my work schedule, Emery and his son, Pat, accompanied by a couple of other adventurers, outfitted a caravan and after some weeks of varied adventure managed to get to the waters of Scammon's Lagoon. They had one boat which at times they had to drag through sand a foot or two at a time, using two automobiles in tandem—a four-wheel drive pick-up and a jeep. They spent so much time getting down there that they didn't do more than hit the high spots when they got there. They had only one boat and one rubber raft.

While they were there they did, however, learn of the beach between Scammon's Lagoon and Guerrero Negro. This beach is the Sargasso Sea of the Pacific, only it is on dry land.

That statement needs a little explaining.

South of Scammon's Lagoon, a range of mountains projects out some forty or fifty miles into the ocean, forming a huge crescent-shaped sickle, and somehow manages to turn one branch of the southbound ocean current in the Pacific into a huge eddy.

Driftage from all over the Pacific Ocean is siphoned into this current, swept around in a huge circle and brought down into this collecting basin. During periods of storm or high wind it is washed ashore. The peculiar thing is that since this shoreline is building up at the rate of half a mile every few hundred years, the wreckage, once caught, is trapped in low, drifting sand hills which can completely cover it within

A catchall for driftage.

a relatively short time, but, conversely, they can, in turn, be blown away by vagaries of the wind, until almost every week sees some new wreckage covered up, some old wreckage uncovered.

According to Emery, no human being had set foot on this stretch of beach within modern times. On the ocean side it is pounded by a terrific surf. On the land side it stretches back in mile after mile of soft sand: hills of sand blown into odd-shaped dunes and at times swept by winds which drive the blowing particles of sand against the skin in a stinging spray. It is in fact a huge triangular-shaped island of sand.

On the north is Guerrero Negro, the "Black Warrior" Lagoon. On the south is Scammon's Lagoon. Landings can be made on the north and south ends of this island but only with a small boat, and the physical problem of transporting supplies across these intervening miles of barren sand is insurmountable.

Scientists from the Scripps Institution of Oceanography, who have been studying the ocean currents, are intrigued by this vast catch basin lying between Scammon's Lagoon and Guerrero Negro. Surveys from the air and the plotting of ocean currents on paper convinced them that here was a beach which held some of the most fascinating wreckage in the world.

Moreover, the British Government recently began to take an official interest in the problem because records indicated that a British ship, carrying several million dollars in gold, had been wrecked on a nearby bar and in all probability the wreckage had been washed ashore on this stretch of beach. It was reported that the British Government had started to outfit an expedition to try and salvage this wreckage but had given it up after studying various legal and international complications, plus the problem of how to get men and supplies on the triangular-shaped island.

Part of my fleet of four-wheel drive automobiles.

While my schedule keeps me pretty well chained down, I like to adventure, although my commitments have necessarily kept my recent adventures confined to relatively small doses. I make brief trips into the desert in search of semi-precious gem stones and unusual photographs. I have a couple of very fine boats equipped with powerful outboard motors. I have a whole fleet of four-wheel drive automobiles with which, on occasion, we make brief safaris into the inaccessible desert. But these hurried trips are all short sprints into the wild and back. Years have elapsed since I've really gone on an adventure trip.

Murl Emery pointed out that by combining our equipment we could make a real trip to Scammon's Lagoon. Instead of taking weeks to get down to the waters of the lagoon as he had done on that exploratory trip, we could do it in a relatively short time. He had the benefit of all the experience he had acquired on his initial pioneering trip, and in addition to that he had purchased a newly invented device which was going to revolutionize beachcombing. This was the "Tote Gote."

It's rather difficult to describe a Tote Gote. To the un-initiated—and I am one—it seems to be nothing but a glori-fied scooter, powered by a light gasoline motor. But there is something about it, an automatic clutch and a few other re-finements, which differentiate it from the ordinary scooter and make it possible to take one of these contraptions just about anywhere a man can go on horseback—or at least that was the story as Emery put it up to me.*

The Tote Gote, Emery said, was made for sportsmen. It was made to go over mountain trails. It was made to go just about anywhere, and Emery had satisfied himself that it would go through deep, soft sand such as one would en-counter on the island beach; bearing in mind that during periods of low tide there would be relatively hard-packed stretches of wet sand on which one could even drive an automobile, if he had a car there. However, when the tide changed one would have to return to base camp through deep sand, and the real beachcombing was back in the soft sand of the drifting dunes.

Looking back on it I don't know at just what stage of the game Emery got my initial interest changed to enthusiasm, or my enthusiasm changed to determination. However, he did it.

* Since this was written, several similar devices have come on the market, one of which, the Pak-Jak manufactured in Paradise, Cali-fornia, has such rugged construction and versatility that I have purchased several of these and am now planning another expedition into Baja California to explore places which have up to now been completely inaccessible.

× II ×

WE DECIDE
TO HUNT WHALES

December of 1959 had found me fighting to complete two book-length manuscripts which had to be in New York before the first of the year. In addition, I was working far ahead on Perry Mason television scripts so I could have ten days' or two weeks' freedom from the chains of Hollywood. All of the Christmas and New Year's activities were crowded into a kaleidoscope of action which left me somewhat dazed on the morning of Sunday, January 2, 1960. Not only did I have numerous guests at the ranch but people were dropping in, in droves, to extend holiday greetings and best wishes for the New Year.

I had told everyone I was going to take the bit in my teeth and break away from routine in 1960.

I had said this on New Year's 1950-1951-1952 and so on, every year, until the persons who heard me simply smiled indulgently and asked me how I intended to get away from my business. I would invariably remark, "The hell with business. I'm going to get out and adventure, camp, and have interesting experiences."

My friends would nod acquiescence, exchange surreptitious winks, and, sure enough, every year I'd start postponing my trip until I had "caught up with the urgent matters." Where-upon more urgent matters would come piling in and I'd repeat the same routine the next year.

Sunday, January 2, 1960 was a surprise to everyone including me.

I sat up nearly all night putting the finishing touches on the manuscripts. I left all of my Christmas correspondence, all of my Christmas presents, unacknowledged and piled in the middle of my study. I threw cameras, films and duffel bags in my jeep and I included what was to prove to be one of the most valuable of all the camping possessions I ever acquired—a new Audograph dictating machine powered by transistors and batteries, hardly larger than a camera yet which functioned perfectly through wind storms, sand storms, pelting rains and the flour-fine dust which inevitably follows cars that venture over the dirt roads of Baja California.

I still remember the looks of incredulous surprise on the faces of my guests as I waved a hurried good-bye, and with-out even stopping to shake hands for fear the inevitable tele-phone ring would drag me back, took off in my jeep for Calexico.

The next morning the rest of the expedition arrived and we made rendezvous about noon, picked up last minute sup-plies, made a few minor mechanical repairs and crossed the border shortly before dark.

I was accompanied by two of my secretaries, Jean Bethell, who had been with me on both of my prior trips to Baja California; Peggy Downs, her sister; both of them veteran campers, accustomed to setting up portable typewriters on a fallen log or an up-ended suitcase and batting out notes; and,

Jean Bethell   Peggy Downs

what was more important on a trip of this sort, acting as my eyes and ears, picking up all available information and cramming it into shorthand books so that the data would be available when needed.

Murl was accompanied by his son, Pat, who has inherited from his father all the love of the Colorado River and adventuring in the out-of-the-way places, but who is somehow more bound to civilization than his father.

Both Murl and Pat are rough-and-ready mechanics who can fix just about anything with almost nothing. They have a wonderful father-and-son relationship, understand each other perfectly, and through years of camping in the desert have learned to co-ordinate with the smoothness of perfection.

Our motor transport equipment consisted of two International one-ton pick-ups equipped with four-wheel drive; a jeep station wagon; another covered jeep with a steel cab and extension body. This jeep was also equipped with a power winch. Both pick-ups were towing nineteen-foot Smithcraft, each powered with twin motors and mounted on two-wheel trailers.

We also carried an assorted collection of jacks, shovels, tow ropes, cables, logging chains and similar equipment.

Sam Hicks, my ranch manager, assistant investigator for the Court of Last Resort, assistant photographer and general right hand, who had been with me on the 1948 trip all the way down the peninsula, was in charge of one of the pick-ups and trailers.

And we had the company of my "companero," Joe Gandara, who has accompanied me on many a Mexican adventure, notably the trips into the Barranca del Cobre, the Barranca Urique and through the Tarahumare country. (Some of these adventures were written up in my book, *Neighborhood Frontiers.*)

Pat Emery

Sam Hicks

Joe Gandara
Anita Haskell Jones

29

Joe Gandara knows of my respect for the cultural background of Mexico. Intensely patriotic and loyal to Mexico, he nevertheless realizes the importance of promoting international friendship and he has spent much time with me at my ranch in Temecula, discussing plans for improving international relations between the two countries. He also is eager to promote conditions which will give the American tourist more of an insight into Mexico.

Well-educated, bilingual, a man who is at home either in the best drawing room or the most primitive camp life, Joe Gandara is a great asset to any outdoor expedition. And he is invaluable in Mexico where he has innumerable official contacts, a thorough knowledge of the people, the customs and the laws, and a natural diplomacy.

Some twenty-odd years ago, when I first discovered Baja California in company with a group of yachtsmen, Anita Haskell Jones was one of the parties making the trip. She is a woman who loves adventure, outdoor life and camping and she has accompanied me on many of my later trips, including the expeditions to the barranca country. Ever since that first yachting trip we have remained warm friends. So Anita was included in this expedition.

This was rather a large party for the type of expedition we had in mind, but at the last minute it was augmented by still another member who was a complete tenderfoot as far as Baja California was concerned.

Some time in December, the editors of *Newsweek* advised me that they wanted to carry a feature article on me starting early in January, but the magazine wanted a little different approach than that of some of the other biographical articles which had been published. The editors telephoned, stating that they wanted to send a reporter down to interview me early in January.

I explained this would be impossible because I was going

to be on an expedition to Scammon's Lagoon in Baja California on that date. The editors immediately became enthusiastic. This was just the new approach they were looking for. They wanted to send this reporter along with us for the first leg of the journey.

I finally consented, upon two conditions: First, that I would talk with the man before we decided. Second, that it would be all right with my companions.

So Joe Laitin came down to the ranch and we had some extensive conversations, following which I somewhat diffidently put through a telephone call to Murl Emery, who was at the time working one of his mines in the wild spaces of Nevada. I left a message for him to call at the station where he gets gasoline and supplies, and it was a couple of days later that the phone rang and Emery was on the other end of the line.

"What do you want?" he asked, coming to the point at once, in true Emery fashion without any dillydallying.

I explained the situation.

"All right, what do you want?"

"I want to know if you have any objections to this guy going along."

"What sort of a fellow is he?"

"Well," I said, somewhat dubiously, "he impresses me as being a nice guy but he looks pretty young."

"That part's all right," Murl said. "We can put another five years on him awful fast."

"Then it's okay with you?" I asked.

"It's okay with me if it is with you," he said, and hung up.

So I relayed word to Joe Laitin that he could come along for the first leg of the trip. I didn't tell him that Murl Emery had said we'd put another five years on him awful fast.

× III ×

DO WHALES TALK?

Since a lot of this story is going to concern itself with the Pacific Gray Whale we had better take a look at the mammal we're going after.

I don't want to set myself up as an authority on whales. There are altogether too many authorities on whales and they have too many different and completely contradictory ideas.

The full-grown gray whale runs from thirty-five to perhaps forty-five feet in length. He is big and powerful and once the early whalers started hunting him he became one of the most vicious and agile of adversaries. As will be seen a little later, whalers who had hunted all other kinds of whales and taken the dangers in their stride, became so panic-stricken when first introduced to the gray whale in the shallow waters of Scammon's Lagoon that the first whaler into the lagoon had to give up hunting whales, despite the fact the lagoon

The gray whale, a most vicious and agile adversary.

was swarming with them, until a brand new technique of killing whales could be invented.

Yet today the turtle fishermen, who sometimes venture into the lagoon, will scoff at the idea the gray whale is dangerous. They say he never attacks a turtle boat.

Now, this brings us to the intelligence of the gray whale and to the question of whether or not whales can communicate.

The answer is they are intelligent and they probably can, and do, communicate.

Experience has proven this: If you go to Scammon's Lagoon to hunt turtles and confine your activities to turtle hunting, the gray whales you will encounter while there will in all probability be neighborly and give you no trouble.

If, on the other hand, you go there for the purpose of hunting whales—whether it be with harpoon or camera—after you have been there a couple of days and "word gets around" among the whales what you are doing, you had better watch out.

Now, don't laugh at this idea of word getting around among the whales. I don't know how these animals communicate but they certainly have some way of exchanging basic ideas. It is now pretty well established that the porpoise (which is first cousin to the gray whale) has a fairly complete language. Underwater sounds have been tape-recorded which show the porpoise is a remarkably intelligent animal, with a means of communication and methods of orientation which are completely mystifying to human observers and far in advance of anything man has devised, even with all of his progress in the field of electronics.

In short, the porpoise, blindfolded and placed in a tank of water, surrounded by movable obstacles, can in some way find a three-inch button no matter where it is placed in the tank and, at a command, will swim to it and press that button.

Donald Douglas, the famous airplane manufacturer who makes so many planes that bear his name, went down to Scammon's Lagoon two or three years ago with Dr. Paul Dudley White. Their idea was to get the heartbeat of a whale and record it on a cardiograph.

When they first arrived the whales were placid and docile. Donald Douglas, standing in the bow of the boat, moved up on a whale which was basking on the surface and jabbed him with an oar. The whale gave a convulsive shudder and submerged so abruptly that the occupants of the boat were splashed with water.

"Nothing to it!" Douglas gleefully assured Dr. Paul Dudley White. "We'll just take little darts with wires fastened to them and put them in the whales by hand."

They didn't get that close to any more whales. On the other hand, the whales got close to them. After they had been in the lagoon long enough for the word to get around that they were hunting whales, the whales decided to turn the tables.

A whale came charging up to the boat, smashed the rudder to smithereens, knocked off the propeller and bent the drive shaft at a forty-five degree angle—all with one blow of his tail. Then he swam away a little distance, turned around, looked at what he had done, took a deep breath and charged, smashing in the side of the boat.

If it hadn't been for executive ability of a high order and a perfectly co-ordinated effort, those men would have been plunged into shark infested waters. But as it was, they worked with speed and efficiency. They stripped off life preservers, stuffed them into the hole, took a piece of canvas, wrapped it around the outside of the boat, signaled for help and, by frantic bailing, were able to keep afloat until a rescue boat, which had been standing by just in case there should be any trouble, was able to come and tow them into shallow water.

Since Scammon's Lagoon is pretty well populated with large, hungry sharks, one can realize just what a situation of this sort could mean

Back in 1949, Lewis Wayne Walker writing in the magazine, *Natural History,* told of a trip to lagoons where the turtle fishermen, on being advised of printed reports from the old-time whalers that the gray whale was a vicious killer, ridiculed the idea. These turtle fishermen said they had spent their lives on the water and daily saw many whales, and the whales were not at all dangerous.

A few days later, however, after the expedition had started hunting whales with cameras, the "word got around" among the whales and the situation changed abruptly.

These same turtle hunters, who had scoffed at the idea the whales could ever become hostile, came paddling to shore in a panic with a whale in hot pursuit.

The whale had charged them, had actually rammed their boat, but because it was a small, light boat high out of the water and because he hit the stern, he hadn't smashed it but had only given it a terrific shove with his nose.

Fortunately the turtlemen were close enough to shore to make it in time but the angry whale was making passes at them and was only deterred when they speedily reached shallow water.

However, I didn't know all of these things when we started out for Scammon's Lagoon. I learned them afterwards, and the hard way.

We now know that while some of the gray whales stay in southern waters, most of them spend the summers up in the Bering Sea. Then they start to migrate in winter and swim some six thousand miles at an estimated speed of four knots an hour until they arrive at Scammon's Lagoon. There the cow whales have their young every second year; there the males gather and the breeding activity takes place.

The whales are there in numbers shortly after the first of the year, and then around March begin to start back. A few of them remain until the middle of April, and there apparently are some who remain there the year around. But for the most part the whale activities in Scammon's Lagoon are between the first of the year and the latter part of March.

The whales, when born, are fifteen to seventeen feet in length and they are nursed until they reach a length of approximately twenty-five feet when they are weaned. And, contrary to general understanding, the whale is a most intelligent mammal, perhaps one of the most intelligent of all the mammals.

My friend, Willard Keith, who is interested in the "Marineland of the Pacific," has told me the story of how they decided to capture a whale and see if it would be possible to train it to do tricks.

The whales are there in numbers.

It took a lot of figuring but they did eventually capture a whale and got it safely installed in Marineland. There, to their surprise, they found that the whale was a thinking animal that speedily learned a whole series of tricks and could put on a performance which would hold an audience completely spellbound.

Anyone who has seen the performance at Marineland will recognize that the whale can be trained just as an intelligent dog can be trained and can and will do just about anything human ingenuity can think of in the line of tricks.

Among other things, we wanted to find out if the whales in Scammon's Lagoon did any feeding while they were there, and we wanted, if possible, to find out why Scammon's Lagoon as the place the whales selected as the goal of their migration. Why not some other lagoon?

Many of the authorities feel that all of the whale food is in the Bering Sea, that once the whales leave there they go on a virtual fast and live entirely on their blubber until they return north once more. On the other hand, since at least a few of the whales remain in southern waters, it would certainly appear that they do feed, despite the assertion of many authorities to the contrary.

But could we *prove* they fed? Could we get a photograph of a whale feeding?

The whale, an enormous creature many tons in weight, lives on some of the smallest bits of sea life. His method of feeding is simplicity itself. He gulps in huge quantities of water, then closing his mouth, expels the water through sieve-like "teeth," getting rid of all the water but leaving all of the small marine animals trapped in the interior of his mouth.

There is no question that the whales put on a lot of blubber in the Arctic Ocean. By the time they reach Scammon's Lagoon, stay there for a few weeks and start the journey back north, they are not as full of fat as when they arrived. But it would hardly seem that evidence such as that would indicate that a whale could swim some six thousand miles, bear young and nurse the young, or engage in mating activities and then swim some six thousand miles back—at the rate of four knots an hour—all without feeding.

After all, many animals put on a lot of fat just prior to the rutting season and then emerge again considerably emaciated to take up the routine tenor of life.

If, of course, there should turn out to be some particular type of toothsome whale-food in Scammon's Lagoon, the migration might be at least partially explained.

Also, in Scammon's Lagoon there is a peculiar formation of shoals which enables the mother whale to lie in relatively shallow water and give birth to the young. The infant can then raise itself enough to get air.

The whale, of course, is not a fish. Being a mammal it

lives under water by first sucking in deep breaths of air, then diving down into the water and remaining until it feels the necessity of coming to the surface for more oxygen. At that time the whale exhales the moist breath from his lungs, and as that moisture strikes the air it congeals and gives us the familiar "blow" which is indescribably beautiful when seen on a still morning against surrounding hills. At such times the early sunlight will catch the plume of moisture and illuminate it as though it were a fountain rising spontaneously from the sea.

My friend, Dr. Carl Hubbs, who *is* an expert on whales, has been quoted as saying that he has repeatedly watched groups of whales, separated by a distance of as much as a quarter-of-a-mile, performing maneuvers with a timing which seems to him most unlikely to be coincidental. He is well aware of the possibility that the whales do have some method of communication. He thinks it is quite possible. In fact, just about everyone who has spent any time with the whales feels certain that somehow or other they can exchange ideas.

As mentioned above, we were blissfully ignorant of all this as we started our expedition down Baja California to photograph the whales in Scammon's Lagoon and to explore many miles of "virgin" beach.

We did, however, feel certain there would be adventures in store for us. There are always adventures in Baja California and, after all, we were looking for adventure. If we hadn't wanted to find it we'd have stayed at home.

So we crossed the border, filled with high spirits, and despite the fact we were intending to take *two* huge nineteen-foot metal boats over the country on two-wheeled trailers, we had a happy-go-lucky "Scammon's Lagoon or bust" attitude; and more or less secretly each one of us hoped that things wouldn't go too smoothly. We wanted an opportunity to cope with the unexpected.

× IV ×

A QUICK LOOK AT
BAJA CALIFORNIA

At this point it might be well to take a quick look at the physical geography of Baja California.

It is a long, narrow peninsula, around a hundred miles at its widest point and not much more than fifty miles wide at its narrowest point. It stretches many hundreds of miles south of the border, down below the Tropic of Cancer, an airplane distance of perhaps eight hundred miles and by road a distance of around twelve hundred miles, if one can call it a road.

Tijuana is a border port of entry. It has many of the characteristics of a rough border town. We are prone to hear altogether too much about the vice of Tijuana and attach the blame to Mexico, little realizing that Mexico furnishes the territory but the United States furnishes the vice. That is, it furnishes the customers without which vice cannot flourish.

40

A QUICK LOOK AT BAJA CALIFORNIA

People should not think of Baja California in terms of Tijuana. Tijuana is isolated. Its tentacles attach to the United States to the north and it is supported by tourists who take the brief half-hour excursion from San Diego which gets them into Mexican territory, geographically speaking, and by those other indivduals who go to Tijuana for the bull fights, races and other things.

Ensenada lies some seventy miles of well-paved road to the south of Tijuana. Here one begins to encounter the real charm of Mexico and its distinctive atmosphere. The American who reaches Ensenada is in search of fishing, of relaxation, of boating in sun-swept waters, of enjoying the beauty of incomparable marine scenery along an ocean drive, of meeting charming, soft-spoken, courteous people, and beginning to get the feel, the atmosphere of old Mexico.

A hundred-odd miles to the east, Mexicali is another border city which is just across the line from Calexico.

Mexicali is entirely different from Tijuana.

Mexicali is the capital of the northern state of Baja California. It is a city of homes and factories.

Baja California is unbelievably picturesque.

There was a time when Mexicali also was a city of vice, but those days have long passed. The Mexicans, with a stern iron hand, have cleaned up the place. As the resorts of vice were torn down, beautiful houses sprang up, industry began to move in. The surprised Mexicans found legitimate business was vastly more profitable than vice had ever been.

Somehow the erroneous impression has permeated the United States that the Mexican is lazy.

The Mexican peon is a creature of infinite patience. If there is work to be done, he does it methodically, unhurriedly and steadily. And he gets it done. If there is no work to be done, he waits. He waits as he works—patiently.

The high-class Mexican is a creature of dynamic energy and of iron nerves. I have seen public officials in their Mexican offices subjected to strain that would wreck the nerves of any American businessman I know. I have watched these officials dispose of a steady stream of people, reaching almost instantaneous decisions, giving orders, making suggestions; firm, courteous, just, sending people away with the feeling they have been treated fairly.

Frankly, I don't know how they do it. I am supposed to be a human dynamo, but I couldn't do it.

I have some friends in Mexicali who are always branching out into new businesses, are always successful. While some people like to hold up the United States as a bugaboo to Mexico, referring to it as the "Colossus of the North," I have been kidding my friends in Mexico recently by expressing fear of the "Colossus of the South."

South of Mexicali there is a large area of fertile farming land. A well-paved fast road runs through this farming land a hundred and twenty-odd miles to the south, to the little fishing port of San Felipe.

San Felipe is on the Gulf. Ensenada is on the Pacific Ocean. They are separated by a high range of mountains. A

Sand drifts up the sun-baked mountains.

Speed is forgotten on these roads.

dirt road winds through these mountains connecting the two cities.

To the south of Ensenada there is a stretch of agricultural land and some improved highway. To the south of San Felipe there is a road which can be traversed by the ordinary car in good condition, to a little place on the Gulf bearing the name of Puertecitos.

This country is unbearably hot in summer but attractive in winter. It is on the Gulf side, with blue waters, alive with fish, to the east, and barren, desolate mountains of sun-baked rock all but devoid of vegetation, to the west.

Beyond Puertecitos adventure starts.

The man who goes more than a few miles to the south of Puertecitos had better have a four-wheel drive automobile, or at least a pick-up with a four-speed transmission. He must have some knowledge of rough road driving and he must have a certain amount of courage. He will also need drinking water, provisions and plenty of gasoline reserves.

For a distance of twenty miles or so the road goes up and down in short pitches. These grades are not over a few hundred feet in height, but they *are* steep. And these steep pitches are very, very rough in places.

The fact that this road can be dangerous is attested to by the remains of battered automobiles which have snapped axles or whose brakes failed, throwing them out of control. Occasionally, one will see the ruins of a loaded truck down at the bottom of the canyon to the side of one of these grades and a wooden cross indicating that the road had taken its grim toll.

On such occasions salvage operations will be performed with a rescue truck. Everything that can possibly be removed will be taken and, in the end, there will be nothing left except bits of splintered wreckage and the wooden cross.

Yet the man who is experienced in driving over rough

Beneath the wooden cross.

roads, who has a sturdy four-wheel drive automobile in good condition, can take this trip without giving it a second thought.

There is one warning. A man should not be in a hurry on the roads in Baja California. If he is in a hurry, he won't get there at all.

In some ways the land has not changed much in recent years. In other ways, it has.

Since my first trip in 1947 many changes have been made in the road. Much of the road has been improved, although the less rugged portions remain as they were.

There is one place where a great change was made. And that was at the most dangerous point on the road, a place referred to in my earlier book as "The Point of the Picture of Death."

This was where the road made an abrupt turn around a

45

rocky promontory shortly before entering Coyote Bay to the south of Mulege. Mexican travelers had painted a skull and crossbones on a projecting rock just before the road came to this point. It was a grim warning.

The road was narrow. It made a sharp turn with a straight drop to the sea on one side and an overhanging rocky wall on the other. The road had literally been blasted out of the rock and was in the nature of a half-tunnel. That is, the wall of rock directly above the road made a jagged overhang. This overhang was so low that when I first encountered it in 1947 there was some doubt that the top of the cab on the Dodge power wagon which I was driving would clear it.

One of our party was seriously injured at this point, despite our precautions. Within a few months the territorial government started work on The Point of the Picture of Death. Much of the overhanging rock was blasted away, the turn

Typical plants in Baja California.

was made less sharp and the road was widened. The picture of the skull and crossbones remained.

Thereafter, from time to time the road has again been widened and improved.

I have derived a certain amount of amusement from reading the accounts of writers who subsequently made the trip over this road, and who somewhat patronizingly referred to my alarm at The Point of the Picture of Death. No person who made that trip prior to 1947 (and there were very, very few) ever referred lightly to The Point of the Picture of Death.

Nowadays, writers who are traversing Baja California are legion. One meets them quite frequently in the northern part of the peninsula, headed south with optimism and various types of equipment. Asking them where they are going, one almost invariably receives the breezy reply that they are going to La Paz.

Three hundred miles farther south one encounters but few of these caravans. Most of the optimistic La Paz travelers have turned back.

Even today very few adventurers drive the long road to La Paz, despite the fact that it has, for the most part, been greatly improved.

× V ×

WE FIGHT OUR WAY
TO GUERRERO NEGRO

It is a long, tedious drive for the hundred and twenty-odd miles from Mexicali to San Felipe but the road is paved and, except for a ten-mile stretch which is a little rough, is in good condition.

Tired and cold (there was no heater in my jeep), we stumbled into the modern motel which had been erected there and went into the dining room lighted by electricity and were given menus which included everything from steaks through all of the standard Mexican dishes to fish which had been freshly caught and tastefully prepared.

We had a delicious meal, then slept until well after daylight the next morning, secure in the realization that at last we had escaped the tentacles of the telephone.

Then we went out and bought Mexican rolls.

I don't know what secret recipe the Mexicans use in mak-

Away from telephones at last.

ing their rolls. All I know is that they have a wonderful flavor and the bakery at San Felipe makes some of the best rolls I have ever tasted. Whenever I have been there I have made it a point to lay in a supply of these rolls and this time we put in bag after bag, fitting them somehow into the load.

Then we were off for Puertecitos.

Because we were taking along two nineteen-foot boats on trailers, there had been an irresistible temptation to load up the boats with various and sundry articles until we had somewhere around a thousand pounds in each boat. In addition to that we had two pick-ups loaded to capacity with gasoline, drinking water, grub, tents, sleeping bags, portable typewriters and cameras.

We made the fifty-three miles to Puertecitos uneventfully. Then we went a few miles on beyond Puertecitos and made camp by the ocean.

The next day we had our first taste of bad roads and of the adventure which seems always to lie in wait along the bad stretches of road of Baja California.

We came to a steep grade, then found a car blocking the road about halfway up the grade.

These grades take just a little more explaining. When I say they are steep, I mean that they are steep. They *can* be negotiated, as I have mentioned, with cars that have only two-wheel drive but usually it takes at least a pick-up with a four-speed transmission to make it; and only a four-wheel drive car gives one a proper sense of security in tackling those grades.

However, because so many pick-ups with two-wheel drive have made passes at these grades and have got stuck up near the top and have spun their wheels, thereby digging holes, the really steep parts of the road are almost unbelievably rough. A driver with a four-wheel drive car can crawl up them satisfactorily. Any other car must make a run for it

Our first taste of bad roads.

and then start pouring on the gas. The result is that riding the steep parts of these roads in two-wheel drive cars is very much like riding a bucking bronco.

This particular car that was blocking the road was a jeep station wagon but it wasn't equipped with the four-wheel drive. The Mexican driver had made repeated passes at the steep grade, had failed every time he tried, and each time had been forced to back down the grade for a new attempt. Finally, he gave up.

The man's wife and two children were with him, and he had quite a few supplies in the car. Right at the start he lightened the car by carrying all his supplies to the top of the hill. He neatly spread a blanket on the ground for his wife and children and they sat there waiting for help. The driver was careful to park his car in the middle of the grade in such a way that no other car could get around it. Then he sat there waiting. There was nothing else to do. He might wait a few

51

hours, he might wait all day, all night and all the next day. He might have to wait for two days.

These things are common in Baja California.

Then, unexpectedly, our caravan came along.

Since our pick-ups were towing the trailers it was decided that my jeep would be the one to act as tow car, and so we got the other car to a place where I could inch around it, and tackled the job.

Trying to tow a car up these rough, steep roads can be quite dangerous. If the man in the car behind loses his head or does the wrong thing, if he lets slack accumulate in the tow ropes so that there is a jerk, all sorts of problems can result. The grades are too steep to drag up a car that is only dead weight, and if the other driver has his power on, there are places in the road where he might go a shade faster than the car ahead and so present the dangerous problem of slack in the tow rope.

Much to my relief my Mexican driver was very skillful and a good tow. I got him over the bad places in the road and up to the top without incident. My jeep didn't even take a long breath, it just buckled down to work and pulled him along.

Up at the top we came to a stop. The family of the Mexican was all but delirious with joy. The driver jumped out of the car, unhooked the tow rope, then ran to embrace his wife and his children. Everybody was laughing and crying at once.

I drove my jeep on for about a hundred feet and then, moved by some premonition, drove it off the road to the edge of a steep canyon, put it in compound low gear, put on the brakes, shut off the ignition, got out and put rocks at the front wheels.

I was just adjusting the second rock when there was a bang that made the jeep shudder as though it had been hit by a cannon ball.

Since my Jeep was unencumbered,
we used it as the tow car.

I was knocked to one side and looked up to see the head-lights and radiator of the jeep we had just rescued looming directly above me. Fortunately it had come to a dead stop.

It seemed that in the delirious excitement of the moment after all their fears of being marooned on the road for several days had subsided, the Mexican had jumped out of his car and embraced his wife and children. He had forgotten to leave the car in gear or to put on the brakes. While the family were embracing and laughing and crying with sheer joy and relief, their car had started to move.

The rest of my party, arriving at that exact time, had dashed after the moving car but it had gained momentum and was headed for the deep canyon. There was only one way to stop it and that was to run it into my jeep, hoping that my brakes would hold. Laitin made a desperate grab through the open window of the car, caught the steering wheel and held on long enough to give it the twist that would head the runaway car in the general direction of my parked jeep.

My brakes, the compression of the motor and the rocks under the wheel held beautifully. My jeep was like the Rock of Gibraltar. The jeep station wagon hit it a terrific blow and everything stopped. The station wagon stopped and my tail light, smashed into a mass of crumpled metal and broken glass, stopped. One fender on the jeep station wagon proceeded to give up the ghost; otherwise, no harm was done.

Tears and smiles of jubilation changed again to near hysteria as far as the woman and children were concerned, but the Mexican, when faced with misfortune, became as calmly competent as a veteran sea captain in a storm. He immediately got busy separating the cars, trying to salvage the fender, pulling it up so it didn't rub against the front tire, and this time blocking all four wheels securely with rocks.

All I wanted was to get the hell out of there before something else ran out of control and into me from behind.

We helped get them loaded and then started them on ahead of us so that if they should have any more trouble we'd be coming along behind where we could give them a lift— and so he'd be up in front where he'd be a problem rather than a risk.

As it turned out, that was the only grade which the husky little station wagon couldn't negotiate. It got by all of the others under its own power.

It seems simply incredible that Mexicans can transport merchandise over these roads by truck. Yet they do it. However, there is quite a percentage of mortality among the trucks. For instance, the next time we came along this particular stretch of road a truck had just gone out of control and plunged over the bank. We looked down on a mass of gasoline drums, beer, soda water, provisions, flour and canned goods; all of the luxuries of civilization which must be freighted in were scattered about in a manner which makes one realize the tragedy of the loss.

The Mexicans who operate these trucks are, for the most part, working on a shoe string. They load the trucks to capacity. The roads are so narrow they can't have dual treads but they do get the most expensive durable tires that money can buy. For the rest, they keep the truck running with ingenious homemade repairs, baling wire and hope. On the tires, however, there is no question of economy. Most of the trucks never start out on those roads unless equipped with the best tires manufacturers can devise.

Here and there people grow the staples. They keep goats and sometimes chickens. But all the luxuries must be trucked in over roads that only a Mexican truck driver has the skill and the will to negotiate. When a truck is lost, which is a not infrequent occurrence, it represents dire economic tragedy to the owner and usually death to the driver.

Lunch time.

Yet they carry on.

Some forty-odd miles below Puertecitos the road turns abruptly and starts up through a long sandy wash toward a level plain at the edge of the granite country. This is a long, steady pull, the soil is fertile but dry and sandy, and yet, except for the fact that it is an uphill grade on a sandy pull, the road is fairly good.

Here the country was literally carpeted with wild flowers.

The season of 1959-1960 was one of the wettest winters Baja California has ever known—and we were destined to feel the impact of the weather.

Down at Scammon's Lagoon where we were headed there is a normal annual rainfall of about one-half of an inch. Now there had been seven inches in the last two months—with more to come, only we didn't know it.

So we crept up the sandy road carpeted with wild flowers until we came to the granite country.

56

The indigenous elephant tree.

Elephant tree swelled with moisture.

HUNTING THE DESERT WHALE

It is impossible to describe this granite country in words and it is exceedingly difficult to get photographs which tell the story of this vast expanse of weatherworn granite, lying silent in the sunlight; a country of mountains, deep canyons, native palm trees, elephant and cirio trees.

Both the elephant and the cirio trees are found in Baja California. I think there is no other place in the world where the cirio tree grows. The elephant tree has crept north into the extreme southern desert section of California, but these trees are indigenous to Baja California.

The cirio tree looks like a huge parsnip when it grows up straight. It has a cone-shaped trunk with branches that normally are only a few inches in length and are covered with green leaves. However, the cirio tree does all sorts of weird

The cirio tree can grow straight.

. . . or bend into
blossoming curves.

. . . or assume
weird shapes.

things. At times it blossoms out into a star at the top. At times this star turns into half a dozen long branches growing straight up like a huge Roman candle. At times the cirio puts out limbs that twist and turn, and at times the whole tree itself for no known reason will bend until it is like some huge, grotesque elephant's trunk.

The elephant tree is a stubby tree with light-colored bark, reminding one somewhat of an elephant's skin, and regardless of the height it attains, it always leaves the impression of stubby strength. It seems to get close to the ground so as to brace itself. The arid region in which it grows has most of its water in the form of brief torrential showers, followed by drought. The elephant tree greedily stores water until it seems to be suffering from dropsy. The bark is pale and wrinkled, the trunk is swollen and stubby, yet the overall effect is one of rugged strength and great beauty.

Up in the granite country winds laden with drifting sand from the lower levels have carved the huge granite boulders near the summit into grotesque shapes; sometimes creating

The granite country.

wind caves in them, sometimes making holes and arches completely through the rocks. Lower down in the wind-protected areas the granite has weathered out until there are times when it seems some giant hand has baked a loaf of granite bread, weighing several thousand tons, and then has sliced it into five or six pieces.

This country is fertile, despite the granite ledges. Ocotillo, cirio, elephant trees, the bisnaga cactus, and much of the smaller desert foliage grow in profusion. The granite casts weird shadows and the dazzling sunlight is so intense in the dry air that these shadows seem jet black by contrast.

This is the home of the famous Baja California big-horn sheep, of deer, of rattlesnakes, and occasionally springs of poison water. It is a country which lies quiet in the sunlight, yet there is a strange power about it.

After the road leaves the flower-covered desert it winds for several miles along the edge of the granite country, then comes to a flat mesa where recently a venturesome individual started making adobe bricks, apparently for no other reason

The home of Baja California bighorn sheep.

Holes worn in the rocks by sand-laden winds.

Granite boulders tumbled in confusion.

than that there was a deep well with plenty of sweet water and lots of suitable soil. The bricks were to be sold at Gonzaga Bay.

There are mines up here and there is a lot of gold in the country.

Near the deep well one can usually find a hard-bitten miner making his headquarters and mining gold from some secret source, extracting the gold from the rich ore by the most primitive of methods and so making enough to live on but not much more.

We make it a point to carry a few luxuries for gifts to people such as these: cigarettes, perhaps a few oranges or tomatoes, bread and matches. These are luxuries beyond price in an isolated country.

These men are deserving. They are glad to receive such gifts as tourists can bring, but they are not moochers. Nor are they beggars. They are men who are eager to find some way of earning a living.

The Mexican who has a little corner of ground can grow

There is a lot of gold in the country.

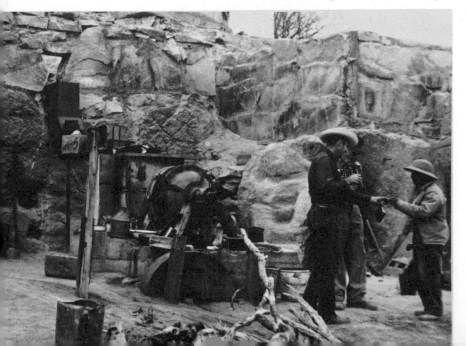

corn, keep goats, and manage an existence. The Mexican who doesn't have these things must have a job if he is going to support himself and in parts of the country jobs are very hard to find. So the ingenious laborer who wants to work but can find no employment, devises various schemes by which he can eke out an existence.

Here and there one will find volunteer road laborers; men who walk out into the places where the road is the most dangerous, make a camp of sorts and voluntarily go to work on the road, trying to keep it in some sort of repair.

Grateful drivers will from time to time leave them cigarettes, perhaps a loaf of bread or a handful of frijoles.

These laborers gratefully accept whatever is offered and continue their work on the road, living in a primitive manner which is almost unbelievable.

We came on one of these camps where the shelter had been formed simply by taking the hood of a wrecked truck,

A hard-bitten prospector.

The primitive camp of volunteer road workers.

. . . constructed mainly around the hood of a wrecked truck.

propping it up on end with stones, to give shelter on the windward side, and then putting cloth on the other side, weighing the cloth down with stones and so furnishing a partial shelter in which two men could find a little protection from the weather.

This camp was as neat as a pin; well kept, and the men were alert and intelligent. They were twelve miles from the nearest place where supplies could be obtained. After receiving a few pesos from grateful truck drivers, they would cheerfully walk the twelve miles to exchange their pesos for a few of the bare necessities of life, then walk back; covering the twenty-four miles in a day, carrying their meager supplies in a small sack. The next day at daylight they would be out working on the road.

And yet, somehow, there is a feeling in the United States that the Mexican is lazy.

Here were men who had created their own jobs; who worked hard; who lived under the most primitive conditions; who never had quite enough to eat; yet who kept themselves clean and presentable; who maintained a spotless camp and who were eager to be of service.

Working only with somewhat battered shovels and a pick, without even the aid of a wheelbarrow, these men were limited as to over-all efficiency. Yet they did the best they could and the truck drivers, themselves working on a slender margin and beset by financial troubles, nevertheless recognizing the spirit of the volunteer road workers gave them a peso now and then or bits of food which the truck drivers themselves could ill spare.

It is that spirit of friendly co-operation, of courteous recognition of a person's intentions, the desire to live and let live, which is so characteristic of Baja California.

Leaving the flat mesa we descended once more into the granite canyons and made camp that night at the site of an

Next morning we hurried on our way.

old mine.

The next morning we were on our way past Lake Chapala, which was now filled with water, and turned south on the road to Punta Prieta.

This is some of the most photogenic country in the world. There are miles and miles of mountains and valleys. Drifting cloud shadows soften the scenery. There are veritable forests of agave, yucca, cirio, elephant trees, the huge cardon, the various varieties of cholla cacti and other desert plants.

And over it all is the cloak of complete silence.

Here one has turned his back on the clock. There is unhurried peace and silence. During the night there will be the hoot of an occasional owl, the weird cacophony of the coyotes; but during the daytime one encounters only brooding silence.

It is impossible to account for the charm of this country or its fascination, but those who are familiar with the land of

Over all is the cloak of silence.

Baja California are either afraid of it or they love it, and if they love it they are brought back by an irresistible fascination time after time.

That night we camped south of Punta Prieta. It was Thursday night and we were still a day and a half from the salt works where there had recently been installed a ship-to-shore telephone service which could be used in periods of emergency for long-distance calls.

The representative of *Newsweek* had been instructed to get in touch with the office by telephone, at least by Saturday morning. When he tried to point out that that might be difficult, they had told him, nonsense, there were always telephones available, to go and make the trip but to be sure to report by telephone Saturday morning.

We couldn't possibly get to the salt works at Guerrero Negro before Saturday afternoon, but Murl Emery pointed out that Pat could take my four-wheel drive station wagon, drive all night, and get there sometime Friday.

Pat Emery was willing, so he, Joe Laitin and Joe Gandara threw some sleeping bags into the jeep station wagon and took off. We made camp and had a good night's sleep.

On arising we found that a smoked turkey we had taken along was beginning to show signs of mildew, so we re-smoked it in a homemade smoking tent, had breakfast, checked the cars and went on.

We had one more night's camp and then arrived at the salt works shortly after noon on Saturday.

We found that Joe Laitin had made his telephone contact with the magazine. The only question they had asked him was the model of the Oldsmobile I was driving at home!

Charles J. McClaughry, the manager of the salt works, is a remarkable executive. He has managed to instill in all of his employees an innate dignified courtesy which permeates the place and gives one the impression that here is no soulless

Charles J. McClaughry, a remarkable executive.

corporation exploiting the native laborer on the one hand and the resources of the country on the other, but a dignified, cohesive body of men all co-operating to the utmost to attain several objectives: profits for the owners, high wages for the men who work there, better working conditions, and, above all, an awareness of human dignity and the rights of the individual.

Truck drivers wave to each other in passing, working men gravely lift their hats to each other as well as to visitors and smile a greeting. Throughout the place is an air of friendliness, co-operation and efficiency.

I know nothing whatever about gathering salt or the complicated mechanics of maintaining water at the exact temperatures where the different chemicals are precipitated, but I do know something about human nature in the aggregate, and I have been in enough factories, company communities and other gatherings to get the feeling of tension where it exists.

I have never encountered any place where there was more of a feeling of cohesive co-operation and an underlying appreciation of human dignity and human rights than here at this salt works, and I feel certain from what I have learned that the mainspring of all this—the inspiration—is Charles J. Mc-Claughry. And his wife has been indispensable in creating a social life in the place.

I suppose this sounds like extravagant praise, but anyone who has been privileged to see the way life goes on at the salt works, and who has been in enough company-owned mining towns or lumbering villages, will know how easy it is for these little communities to become hotbeds of petty jealousies on the one hand and sullen routine on the other.

Of course, McClaughry must have had good basic raw material to work with. You can't make a silk purse out of a sow's ear, but all human beings have a desire to bring out the best that is in them and McClaughry has implanted this as an ambition in his various employees there at the salt works.

To me it was an inspiration to see a one-company settlement maintained in this manner.

We were given permission to use the company road across the salt pans and down to the gauging station on Scammon's Lagoon. This is the only road by which automobiles can reach Scammon's Lagoon. The road traverses some eighteen miles of sand and salt.

We found the salt pans flooded. This flooding was not the result of design but was due to the fact that enough rainfall to cover an average for some fourteen years had fallen in the last two months, raising problems in connection with production which were becoming increasingly serious. When a salt pan has been flooded for just the right period it suddenly starts dissolving and turns to mush with startling rapidity. At such times an automobile striking a soft spot could sink out of

71

When we first crossed the salt pans,
the water was only a few inches deep.

sight very quickly if immediate help was not available.

We found that the salt pans we must cross had been flooded for some time and there was a question whether we would be trapped if we had to cross them many times.

When we first crossed these salt beds the water was only a few inches deep but it had been fresh water which had been standing there for some time. Under the circumstances, there was the natural tendency to hurry across so we could get safely to the other side—and hurrying is just the wrong thing to do.

Not only is it a mistake to hurry across the submerged salt pans, but it is a mistake to try to hurry anywhere in Baja California. A speed of six or seven miles an hour across the salt pans will get you where you want to go; but it is a great temptation to increase speed to twelve or fifteen miles an hour. Then the churned-up salt brine is splashed over the undercarriage of the car, over the springs and spring shackles and some of the drops may get caught by the fan and thrown against the distributor.

Heaven help you if this salt brine ever gets in the ignition!

After you are across the salt pan the water dries and leaves an encrustation of salt all over the car. Later on, whenever you encounter moist air, particularly on a dewy night, the salt will attract the moisture and if the salt has got to the ignition system, the resulting condensation will cause conditions which will prevent the car from starting.

I made the mistake of going a little too fast, not across the salt pan itself but through one of the puddles in the road which, as it turned out, was encrusted with salt. Water got into the ignition of the jeep, and since it was only a hundred yards from camp I walked away and left the car. I returned after a couple of hours when the water had dried off and it started without trouble.

After that, however, whenever there would be a heavy dew

at night, my jeep simply wouldn't start in the morning until it had been dried out by hand and then towed along behind another car.

As it happened, we crossed the salt pans this first time in good shape, fought our way through the sand hills beyond and came to the gauging station at the end of the road where we were going to make our first camp.

Ahead of us lay the waters of Scammon's Lagoon and we made camp right on the brink of the lagoon.

× VI ×

THE STORY OF
SCAMMON'S LAGOON

The story of Scammon's Lagoon is completely fascinating, just as the story of Charles M. Scammon, the man after whom the lagoon was named, is a fascinating story of Yankee ingenuity, of the early days of whaling and of the shameful destruction of natural resources.

There is some conflict among the authorities as to just how Charles Scammon discovered his private hunting ground. In fact, when it comes to whales and whale hunting, the authorities seem to be pretty generally in conflict.

One authority has it that Scammon befriended a Chinese sailor in Honolulu, that this Chinese had been exploring the coasts of the United States and Mexico in a Chinese junk and offered to guide Scammon to a veritable hunting paradise in return for Scammon's kindness.

The other account is that Scammon, using the remarkable

Gandara finds a whale bone.

powers of observation which he undoubtedly had, obtained clues pointing to the fact that somewhere along the west coast of Baja California there was a place where whales congregated. However, so cunningly is the entrance to Scammon's Lagoon concealed that, despite the fact he was searching for such an entrance, he sailed by it without seeing it.

An alert look-out, however, at the top of the mast, taking his attention from the ocean and observing the long, low sand hills, was surprised to see the spouts of several whales coming apparently from a rolling, sandy desert.

Quite obviously whales do not spout on dry land. Despite the fact the look-out felt he was looking over miles of arid desert and low, rolling sand hills back of an unbroken line of surf, the unmistakable fact was that once attention was directed toward dry land there were plainly visible the spouts of numerous whales appearing over the low sand hills—proof positive that there must be a lagoon.

Scammon had a large vessel and a smaller vessel. He anchored the larger vessel, lowered two whale boats, and sent the whale boats and the smaller vessel looking for a channel into the lagoon. It took them two days and two nights before the whale boats were able to return with the statement that a channel had been located and the cutter was already in the lagoon.

One marvels at the fortitude of these men who took to the oars and spent two days and two nights in open boats exploring an unknown, dangerous coast line. And after one has realized how tricky the channel to Scammon's Lagoon really is; how necessary it is to get inside the surf line and then come on back inside a dangerous bar and parallel the surf-washed shore of an island, one wonders that the men were able to find this channel at all.

But the men did find it, and after some maneuvering Scammon got his big boat into the lagoon and they were ready to start whaling.

As mentioned previously, they took two whales without incident but the next day when they went whaling it was a different situation. The whales seemed to know exactly what was wanted and avoided the boats wherever possible but, when crowded, promptly turned and attacked. And the whales were so agile, so vicious and so powerful that they were christened "the devil fish."

The terminology of whaling is simple, direct, and to the point. For instance, the "Right" whale was so christened simply because the whalers felt he was the right whale to harpoon when there was any choice in the matter. And now the gray whale became known as the devil fish.

After the first few encounters, most of Scammon's men simply refused to man the boats; and when Scammon did get a volunteer crew, the first whale which came toward the boat found every one of the men jumping overboard and leaving the boat unmanned.

The word had got around and the whales were fighting back.

For two days Scammon's crew did no whaling at all, simply trying to ascertain how they could work out a new technique by which these whales could be captured. They were in a veritable whaler's paradise, with whales blowing all around them, but almost half the crew was injured, their boats had been stove in and the whales, seeming to know exactly what the foe was there for, were ready to attack a boat whenever it showed up within range, so to speak.

The carpenters worked long hours getting the broken boats repaired so that they would be sea-worthy.

At length a new scheme was proposed: The boats would anchor in shallow water by the edge of a channel. The whales could not get at them in the shallow water but, as whales came drifting past in the deep channel, one of the guns would fire a "bomb-lance" into the whale, hoping to reach a vital point.

The seasoned whalers felt that this would not work but they couldn't think of anything else that would work so they tried it.

The day they put this plan into execution they fired bomb-lances into three whales. These bomb-lances were ingenious devices, intended to explode after they had penetrated the whale's vitals.

Three whales were killed; two of them sank to the bottom but the crew managed to get a line on the third whale and towed him to the boat. Later on that day the other two bombed whales came to the surface and were found drifting

Emery measuring the skeleton of a gray whale.

with the tide. Lines were promptly attached to them, they were towed to the ship, and Scammon was in business.

Within record time Scammon filled his boat and exhausted his supply of bomb-lances. Getting the loaded boat back out of the bar, however, was a problem. It was more than twelve days before they found conditions of wind and tide which enabled them to take a chance with the heavily loaded boats; and even then they left a trail of sand behind them as they dragged their keels across the bar.

One of the authorities has it that the Scammon boats were part of the whaling fleet out of New Bedford and that they returned to New Bedford. But, judging from the writings of Scammon himself, it would seem that he was working out of San Francisco.

In any event, when the Scammon boats came in loaded to capacity with whale oil and whalebone, there was a lot of speculation.

HUNTING THE DESERT WHALE

Scammon had agreed to keep his crew working on shares, and swore each one to secrecy. So there was no word of Scammon's Lagoon or the new whaling discovery. The feeling was that Scammon had simply been lucky.

In those days the whalers went out and stayed out until they filled their boats. Many of the expeditions lasted for four or five years, with the boats cruising from the Arctic to the Antarctic. So naturally the fact that Scammon was back with a full boat within a matter of weeks was cause for speculation.

Scammon apparently made another trip to his lagoon without arousing any comment. But when he again returned within a few weeks with his boats loaded to capacity, the competitive whalers became suspicious, and when Scammon started on his next trip a whole fleet of whalers was following along, determined to find Scammon's secret whale-hunting grounds.

Scammon's Lagoon, and part of its long, low shoreline.

Scammon would keep in sight of the fleet during the daylight hours, then at night he would double and twist and turn and be out of sight by daylight. But the fleet would scatter and inevitably some of the look-outs would pick up Scammon's sail and again the chase would be on.

Eventually, however, Scammon dodged the fleet and once more entered his secret lagoon and started operations.

The baffled hunters cruised everywhere trying to find where Scammon had disappeared.

In the end it was the wind which betrayed Scammon's location.

A look-out on one of the whaling ships which had been cruising off Cedros Island noticed the telltale taint of whale blubber trying out, and reported to the captain, who promptly turned the ship into the wind and started following the scent which of course kept growing stronger until, to his amazement, the captain beheld the spars of Scammon's ship apparently moored in the middle of a sandy desert; and surrounded by the spouts of whales.

The low sand hills completely masked the lagoon but the spouts of whales some ten or fifteen feet high (and even reaching to twenty feet under proper atmospheric conditions) which had disclosed the lagoon to Scammon, plus the telltale spars of Scammon's ship, betrayed the location to the captain of the other vessel.

But locating Scammon's Lagoon and locating the channel were two different things.

Scammon himself has written that on his next trip while there were some forty vessels standing by outside the surf, only eight of them managed to get into the lagoon.

However, the secret was no longer a secret and these hardy seafaring men soon learned the channel, and the whaling fleet moved into Scammon's Lagoon. They began such a massacre of whales as baffles description.

Reading the accounts of the hardened whalers of those days it appears that they themselves were indescribably shocked by the slaughter, carried on amidst scenes of confusion and violence, with the desperate whales attacking the whalers, with harpoons and bomb-lances flying, and boats so thick that at times lines were crossed and boats being towed by frenzied harpooned whales crashed into each other.

For a few years this slaughter continued and then suddenly the gray whales vanished. It was thought they were all extinct.

Actually, however, the whales had used their intelligence and, apparently as the result of deliberate strategy, had changed their annual migration from California to Korea.

It seems incredible that the whales could have acted in concert in a matter of this sort, yet there is some evidence to support such a theory.

Unfortunately there are not enough accurate records available so that we can tell exactly what did happen, but apparently all at once the whales simply quit returning to the Coast of California and to Scammon's Lagoon. The whalers thought the gray whale had become extinct. However, and at about that same time, the gray whale turned up off the coast of Korea, headed for lagoons and warm waters.

By this time the gray whale had developed a nasty disposition. After the whales had pursued this new route long enough to be recognized, the contemporary writers state that gray whales encountered on the Korean migration were exceedingly belligerent, and this was doubly true of the males, who would attack a boat on sight.

Nor should one doubt the intelligence of the gray whale. They soon began to associate the long row boat, known in seafaring terminology as the "whale boat," with their hunters.

Whalers who worked on the ocean found that as soon as a whale boat was launched the gray whales would vanish but the same was not true when the smaller fishing boats were in the water. And so, for a while, an attempt was made to take gray whales with a very small, light boat, capable of transporting only two people; one person who would scull, and the harpooner, who would wait in the bow.

Within a short time, however, the whales detected this subterfuge and again the word got around. Soon the grays would veer off from the small boats the same as from the larger boats.

Living under present-day conditions, it is very difficult for us to imagine the hardships faced by these rugged whalers who followed the sea.

Now we have auxiliary motors and compact gasoline or Diesel engines. In those days there was no auxiliary power. A sailing ship depended upon the wind, its sails and the skill of its handling.

We have now come to accept electric refrigeration as almost a necessity of life. In those days there was no refrigeration available for those sailors who had to live day after day, month after month, and sometimes year after year on the whalers. They would stop from time to time at ports and pick up drinking water and a few fresh supplies but after a short time these supplies would be exhausted. Meat, in particular, could only be kept "pickled" in brine. There was no cooling system for the drinking water, which quite frequently became foul. When the wind died down a ship was becalmed. It might well be becalmed for a day, two days, or a week.

During those periods the sun beat down upon the deck with fierce intensity. The crew lived on "salt horse" and "hard tack."

Then the whaling ships would follow the whales up into the Arctic, sometimes being caught in the winter ice and either crushed or held a drifting prisoner until the spring thaw.

Men who could face all of these hardships of diet and climate must have been very rugged, very tough and very tenacious.

Reading the early accounts of whalers one is impressed with the risks these men took. Having "darted" an iron into a whale, having let out perhaps a mile of line when the whale "sounded," they would find themselves towed many miles by the anguished creature—towed until they were entirely out of sight of the mother ship which would then have to try and find them.

These men were out in a trackless ocean. The mother ship would perhaps be miles away and getting farther behind all the time. Night would be coming on. The men had to pull the line in by sheer strength, and when one considers the resistance of the water, the slap of the waves and the speed with which the whale was taking them, this becomes quite an operation. Then, having worked in close enough to the whale to reach him with the lance, they tried to stab at the whale's "life." These thrusts with the lance sometimes missed the whale's "life" and so infuriated him that he turned on the boat, smashing it to splinters and leaving crippled men to drown in the ocean.

Such battles required strength, co-ordinated effort, a rare degree of skill and an iron nerve.

Darkness would frequently ensue before the battle was over and sometimes a fog or a storm would complicate the situation so that the mother boat might well lose all track of the crew manning the whaling boat.

Yet men did these things and did them year after year.

Perhaps one of the most impressive things about the history of Scammon's Lagoon is that, after the gray whale had been hunted enough to become aggressive, he was able to inspire terror in men who had nerves of steel and who had followed the whaling business all of their lives.

It is now very difficult to get access to a copy of the book Charles M. Scammon wrote in 1875, entitled *The American Whale Fishery*, but anyone who is able to find this book and read it will get quite a knowledge of whales and will be filled with admiration for the two-fisted, iron-nerved men of the whaling industry.

The slaughter of whales had been so great that when they disappeared scientific writers claimed the gray whale was all but extinct and within a few years would have gone the way of the buffalo. However, as so frequently happens, the prophets failed to take into consideration certain other factors which were destined to exert a great influence. The development of the petroleum industry, the strides of science in connection with refining lubricants, soon literally put the whaling industry on the greased skids, and it was the whaler who became all but extinct. Now the activities of the remaining whalers are so regulated by international agreements that the whales stand better than an even chance of replenishing their numbers.

Following the slaughter of the gray whales in Scammon's Lagoon and the withdrawal of the whalers themselves under economic pressure, the lagoon lay for many years, a virtually unknown body of water, slumbering peacefully in uninterrupted solitude.

After scientists became interested in the ocean and ocean currents, the Scripps Institution of Oceanography, studying the mysteries of the ocean, soon learned that the gray whales were coming back down the coast and returning in numbers to Scammon's Lagoon.

My friend, Dr. Carl Hubbs, started making aerial surveys to take an annual census of the whales in the lagoon. And, as reports were made, the press picked up the information and it soon became known that whales were returning in numbers to their old breeding grounds.

It is to be remembered that the whale is a mammal and is, therefore, in a way, related to man. Man has recently been bothered with a great deal of heart trouble. The heart of man is a very small organ, but the heart of a whale is a huge pumping device weighing up to two hundred and fifty pounds. It was felt that if studies could be made of the heart of the whale and its circulatory system, information might be gained which would be of value to the human race.

Dr. Paul Dudley White, the famous heart specialist, was anxious to secure electrocardiographs of the heart action of a living whale. He enlisted the aid of Donald Douglas and the Douglas Aircraft Company and soon their research boat, the *Dorado,* bearing Donald Douglas and Dr. Paul Dudley White, was headed for Scammon's Lagoon.

I have previously mentioned some of the results of that trip. The "word got around" among the whales and the expedition came limping back with a stove-in power boat and men who had acquired a healthy respect for whales.

The problem of getting an electrocardiograph of a living whale is not a simple one. It is necessary to place two electrodes in the whale; one as near the neck as possible, and the other as near the tail as possible.

Having become interested in the problems of the whale's heartbeat, Donald Douglas really went to work. And the following year he and Dr. White were once more on their way to Scammon's Lagoon. This time, however, the situation was far different from what it had been the year before.

They had been offered the co-operation of the Mexican Government, of the United States Army, and again had the co-operation of the National Geographic Society.

For some months Donald Douglas had been working on the idea of placing electrodes in the whales from a helicopter, and an ingenious power gun had been worked out which would fire twin harpoons simultaneously, spread at just the right angle to penetrate the skin of the whale at head and tail, and designed to furnish maximum electrical contact.

The harpoons had been so fashioned that they would not go deep enough to hurt the whale, and would, in the course of a brief space of time, be dislodged by the muscular actions of the whale.

Wires from these harpoons went to a small boat which was strapped to the bottom of the helicopter. This compact boat was literally packed with batteries and wiring and was so designed that when it hit the water an aerial automatically came up and the electric impulses were sent by wireless from this small boat to a receiving station on the Douglas research yacht, the *Dorado*.

On that expedition they were able to get both of the electrodes in whales and, while the results were not all that they had hoped for, they did obtain much valuable information.

Scammon's Lagoon, which had lain dormant, so to speak, for so many years was now back in the news, and the attention of people throughout the civilized world was fastened upon it.

It should be remembered that the salt works at Guerrero Negro are not a mining operation, as one might at first think. The huge salt pans which have been formed over a period of millions of years by the evaporation of sea water are used merely as a level foundation on which to impound new sea water and harvest this new salt.

Strange as it may seem, the activities of this company result in increasing the deposits on the salt pans, rather than decreasing it. Yet, by the use of scientific equipment and modern machinery, they annually harvest thousands of tons of new salt recovered from the ocean.

As the enterprise prospered it grew in magnitude until now there is quite a settlement at the salt works in Guerrero Negro. A road was constructed across the dry salt pans to the

The shores of Scammon's Lagoon, dotted with wrecks.

head of Scammon's Lagoon where there is a tide gauging station. This road is just about the only way by which wheeled vehicles can get to the borders of the lagoon. It was our intention to launch our boats from the trailers directly into the waters of the lagoon; then to transport our equipment to an island in the middle of the lagoon and there make camp, hauling our drinking water and our gasoline in cans from the mainland to camp.

It is thus seen that the shores of Scammon's Lagoon, dotted here and there with the wrecks of whaling vessels which came to grief, have been through several periods of transition and within the last few years have even heard the whirring of the blades of a helicopter.

And it is now becoming apparent that "word has gotten around" among the whales that they are once more an object of interest. This makes the whales nervous. They can't understand this sudden renewed interest on the part of man, or the peculiar machines which hover high in the air.

Some of the whales will remain relatively calm in the presence of a helicopter. Some will "sound" at the first intimation an object in the air is taking an interest in them. In fact, I have even seen whales sound, apparently in fright, when flying over them in a plane at an elevation of at least five thousand feet.

So far as we know, no other persons had ever invaded the waters of the lagoon with two strong metal boats, each equipped with twin outboard motors capable of making great speed.

This method of whale hunting had advantages, although it also had very great disadvantages. But it offered adventure and the thrill of the unknown; and, very frankly, we wanted to find out just what would happen.

× VII ×

WE ESTABLISH CAMP
AT SCAMMON'S
LAGOON

It was low tide when we first arrived on the banks of Scammon's Lagoon. We couldn't launch our boats until the tide had come in. So we unloaded the pick-ups, made our camp, put the trailers in a position to launch the boats early in the morning when the tide was up, and then spent an hour or two looking the country over.

There was a turtle camp nearby, and a keen-eyed, leathery-faced Mexican who had spent many years making a living from the sea, came out to greet us.

This man, Justo, was quite a character. His right hand was gone. Fishing with dynamite, he had been a little late in tossing the explosive and had lost his hand. We heard afterward that he had made a tourniquet and walked interminable miles to a place where he could get medical help, accepting the misfortune philosophically.*

* Justo had his final misfortune on Good Friday of 1960 when he was drowned in the treacherous waters of Scammon's Lagoon.

**Unloading supplies at Scammon's Lagoon
(Justo's turtle camp in the middle distance).**

Justo had worked and worked hard. He made his one hand do the work of two. He had built up quite a turtle business, and at the moment had a large stock of turtles awaiting shipment.

His method of shipping was to load the turtles in an open boat equipped with an outboard motor and a small standby motor, then take off across the open sea to Cedros Island some thirty miles away. There he could sell his turtles to the cannery.

That afternoon Justo had secured a turtle which he was waiting to take over to his camp. The turtle had been neatly turned on its back, in which position it was completely helpless, and was lying there on the beach.

These turtles make delicious food and, after all, it is the scheme of nature that life must support life; but this was our first close-up meeting with an unfortunate turtle.

Once they are turned on their backs on dry land they can't possibly right themselves. They make futile efforts, then finally give up, settle back and close their eyes, apparently sleeping.

Perhaps it was our imaginations but I am willing to swear that this turtle who was lying on his back asleep and which awakened when I approached, had a second or so during which he was orienting himself and then suddenly his eyes widened and I had the feeling there was an expression of terror in them.

I tried to stroke his throat and reassure him but the only result was to start him struggling helplessly. This time I thought his eyes were pleading for help.

Anyhow, with three women in the party the result was a foregone conclusion.

We hunted up Justo, who owned the turtle, and told him we wanted some turtle meat. He had a turtle right there at the camp and how much would he take for him?

Typical camp of a turtle hunter.

We didn't fool Justo for a minute. He sold us the turtle at wholesale price and because it soon became apparent that we hadn't fooled him we confided in him that what we wanted to do was to turn Mr. Turtle loose and we didn't want him caught again. He was our turtle and as such immune from being netted any more.

Justo quickly understood. There was a twinkle in his eyes as he waded out into the low-tide muck and slime with his rubber boots, turning the turtle over, moistening its back with sea water for apparently a turtle becomes even more helpless once his shell dries out.

I acquired the greatest regard for Justo then and there. The man might make his living by snaring turtles and selling them on the market but he had a big heart and a lot of warm, human sympathy.

He spent almost as much time getting the turtle out into the water, getting him properly wet through, and steered on a course to deep water, as he had spent in catching the turtle in the first place.

Nor did he look at us afterwards with the expression one reserves for rich *Yanqui turistas* who are crazy. He smiled understandingly. One gathered that he would like to turn all of his catch loose if it weren't for the fact that he had to catch turtles in order to live.

We only intended to stay at this camp long enough to get the boats launched, so we hurriedly unloaded the cars, piling everything helter-skelter on the sandy hills above the high water line, and then went out in search of wood.

Firewood in this place was at a premium.

I didn't give the matter any thought at the time. All I knew was that we needed firewood and we had to go some distance to gather it. It never occurred to me in my selfishness to wonder what Justo and his companion at the turtle camp did for their firewood.

Afterwards I found out that getting enough firewood to cook a meal involved much walking and much searching.

A few shrubs grew to a height of six or eight inches above the soil and occasionally some of these died and the wood became dry enough to burn. Justo and his companion would start out in the afternoon with a length of light rope about two and a half feet long. They would be gone for perhaps an hour or an hour and a half and come back with a little bundle of sticks tied up in the rope. This was their firewood.

The fire was hardly bigger than the light of a candle, carefully fed and nursed with the precious wood so that every bit of flame did its share in cooking a meal.

Murl Emery knew of a place up on a bluff some six or seven miles away where there were larger bushes growing and we took the empty pick-ups and went up to this place, returning with a couple of pick-up loads of firewood.

We cooked our supper, spread out our sleeping bags, inflated the air mattresses and built a roaring camp fire.

I have often wondered how Justo and his companion must have felt as they sat by their little candle-sized flame and looked across a couple of hundred yards to where the "rich tourists" had a roaring camp fire some six or eight feet in diameter, sitting around it toasting their bodies and wasting the precious natural resources of the country.

Eventually we let the fire die down but still left plenty of wood for a big breakfast fire in the morning.

It was cloudy but we felt certain it *couldn't* rain. The country was soaked! It had more than enough rain to last for years. According to the law of averages the rains must be over. This was only a high fog.

We drifted blissfully off to sleep.

I wakened about midnight with the first gentle drops falling on my face. I sighed, thought some of getting up to distribute my bed canvas more evenly, but drowsily pulled it up over my head and trusted to luck that it was all right. I went back to sleep and was awakened by pelting rain, pouring down, hitting my bed canvas and running off into the sand.

I was warm, the canvas was keeping me dry. I had nothing to worry about, so once more I didn't take the trouble to get up and see that the folds of the upper canvas were spread out over the lower canvas so that water wouldn't run into my sleeping bag. After all, I reasoned drowsily, this couldn't be any more than a shower.

Rain came down in curtains, in sheets, in torrents. I later found out that the lower canvas had spread out so it was catching the drop from the upper canvas and my sleeping bag was lying in a pool of water. By that time it was too late to do anything about it and I felt certain that the next day would be sunny and warm and I could spread things out and let them dry; so again I drifted off to slumber.

Daylight came; a cold, wet, dismal dawn with rain still pelting down. I stayed in my sleeping bag as long as possible and then finally faced the bitter chore of crawling out of a warm sleeping bag and dressing in the midst of a cold rain.

I squirmed my way out of the sleeping bag and rubbed my eyes in surprise. During the night Sam Hicks and Pat Emery had dressed and put up the big tent in the dark. They had put in a stove, built a fire in the stove, and not only was the tent warm and dry but the water which fell on the top of the tent was turning to steam and evaporating, simply from the warmth of the fire in the stove.

Quite naturally I gathered my clothes and made a run for the tent, only to find that the others had done likewise and soon we were all dressed, waiting for it to let up.

The rain didn't let up. Everything that had been out in the open was soaking wet. So we had the job of launching the boats in the rain, trying to protect our films and cameras as best we could with what waterproofing we had, and fighting our way out across Scammon's Lagoon to the island where we intended to make our camp—all in a drenching downpour.

The reason I mention all this is that the stove didn't use nearly as much wood as the open camp fire. By the time we had had breakfast, had launched the boats, had squeezed as much water as we could out of the things from which water could be squeezed, and had loaded the boats to make the first trip to the island, we still had a lot of firewood left in the pile.

Personally I didn't give this firewood very much thought. I felt that it would come in handy for Justo and his companion, camped over there on the point, but right at the moment my main concern was to try and get to where we could establish a more permanent camp, put up all of our tents and try if possible to get dried out before nightfall.

Rain was the one thing we hadn't counted on. We had, of course, brought tents just in case, but we had expected to use these mainly as shelters against the winds and the heavy dews which are customary at night along the ocean.

Our first boat loads took only the absolute necessities for our new camp: a tent, a stove, some provisions, and some of the photographic material. The rest we covered with canvas and left for a second load.

Therefore it happened that my first experience with the whales in Scammon's Lagoon was during a period of rain, of wind-driven moisture and a cold wind from the ocean.

The island where we were going to make our camp was some fifteen or twenty miles down the lagoon but, even heavily loaded, our boats could make a good twenty miles per hour.

Right at the moment we were not interested in whales.

We were mainly interested in dry clothes and a warm fire.

I remember looking at the pile of wood we had built up and wondering vaguely if there would be wood we could burn on the island, but it would have been out of the question to have tried to add wood to our burden on the loaded boats, so we put just as much of a load in the boats as we felt they would carry for that first trip and shoved off.

The point is that the abandoned wood pile stayed there for some ten days or two weeks. The frugal Justo and his companion came over and cleaned up everything we had left behind which they felt certain we had intended to throw away; an old canteen which had sprung a leak, the empty tin cans which we had buried and which the coyotes had promptly dug up; everything that we had discarded as of no further use to us which Justo and his companion could use they had picked up and carried away.

But the wood pile? When we came back at the end of ten days that wood pile was intact, waiting for us.

That rain turned out to be the forerunner of a three and a half day storm. Justo and his companion must have been cold, wet and miserable. They needed firewood badly. They couldn't go out to get it and there was a pile of abandoned firewood of sufficient magnitude to last them for two or three weeks with their frugal way of living and their conservation of firewood; but the thought of touching it never entered their minds. We hadn't told them they could have it, therefore they reasoned we would probably want it on our return. The fact that we would touch a match to it and burn up a three weeks' supply of firewood in an hour or two didn't have anything to do with it. This was our wood. We had gathered it. They wouldn't think of touching it.

I mention this in order to show something of the inherent honesty of the Mexicans of Baja California. I have encountered this time and time again. I remember one time that we made a camp and carefully buried all of our empty tin cans. Then we started on and for some reason didn't go far before making another camp. A Mexican passed us going down the road, came to our old camp, found the place where we had buried our empty cans, and then turned around and came all the way back riding his burro over several weary miles to ask if we intended to use those cans again or if we had thrown them away, because if we had thrown them away he wanted them very much to use as cooking utensils.

These people lead simple lives. Their wants are few but such wants as they do have are vital. Firewood and cooking utensils are wealth, yet their honesty is such that they would freeze or starve rather than touch something that belonged to someone else.

× VIII ×

WE MEET
OUR FIRST WHALES

The weather lightened a little bit after we got under way. I held one of my cameras under a rainproof poncho, despite the fact that my clothes were wet, and stood in the bow of the boat waiting for the first whale adventure.

It wasn't long before we had it.

A whale unexpectedly came to the surface a short distance in front of our boat, shot out a great cloud of steamy breath and then plunged down to the bottom, thoroughly alarmed by the boats and sending up great disturbances in the water every time his powerful tail propelled him forward.

At the time I didn't know enough about whales to realize that he was getting away as best he could. All I knew was that the water was churning about the boat and I began to wonder vaguely if we could count on these whales being safe.

The whale plunged to the bottom.

A few miles farther on we came on several whales drifting along on the surface of the water. They promptly submerged when Emery's boat, which was in the lead, came within a few feet of them. One of the whales, however, didn't go deep. He remained just under the surface, whirled around past Emery's boat, then, as we could see under the surface of the water, made directly for our boat.

I watched for a moment and didn't like the way he was coming. There was something purposeful about his progress, and he was moving at speed. He was making no attempt to submerge but remained just a few feet under the water, headed directly for us.

"Sam," I said, "I don't know enough about these whales to depend on Emery's judgment. Let's get the hell out of here!"

We had lots of horsepower in that boat and Sam shoved the throttle forward and we got out of there, just a few feet ahead of the approaching whale.

At the time I thought the whale was charging but I didn't venture the opinion because I didn't know anything about whales and I was the only one who seemed alarmed.

Later on, after I got home and started reading about whales I knew darn good and well he was charging.

It was that day I began to realize something of what we were up against in photographing whales.

A whale is an enormous mammal. He is dark in color except where there are patches of white on his skin and where barnacles cling to his hide. He comes up out of the blue water, spouts, and goes down. While he is spouting, only a few inches of his huge body are above the water. Sometimes I doubt if he protrudes more than six inches above the surface.

When you try to take his picture there is little contrast between the whale and the water. If one is standing in a

There is little contrast between whale and water.

boat so that the camera is five or six feet above the waterline there is no way of showing a silhouette of the whale's back that is out of the water.

Moreover, an ordinary focal-length lens will make a whale only a few feet away appear to be quite distant. The long focal-length lens will blur the image on the film because a telefoto lens requires a firm, steady foundation and you can't get a firm, steady foundation in a bouncing small boat.

In fact, as we were to learn later, photographing whales in their native habitat is just about the most difficult photographing assignment one could wish for.

We saw quite a few whales on our trip to the island, but I signaled Emery that I didn't want to deviate our course an inch in order to take whale pictures. We were racing against the tide because once the tide went down we would have to wade across muddy tide flats in order to transport stuff to and from the boats. We had literally hundreds of pounds of equipment, and the fact that much of our camp equipment was soaking wet didn't simplify the problem. A dry tent which weighs a hundred pounds is quite a problem, but let that tent once get wet, getting it transported and put up becomes an engineering feat.

We reached the island and Sam Hicks and Pat Emery worked like Trojans, rushing stuff ashore, putting up a shelter tent and connecting a stove. Then they dashed off in the boats to pick up the rest of the camp and we started trying to gather firewood.

It immediately became apparent that getting firewood was going to be quite a problem. On the island there was a variety of bush which grew several feet off the ground and here and there were some bits of dead brush. But others had camped on the island before us and there was but little firewood, and what little there was, was soaking wet.

After we got the things which we had taken in the boats

on that first trip under cover, I suggested that the only way to keep warm and at the same time conserve firewood was to go walking and keep walking. That way at least we could keep the blood circulating. I had tried it before on rainy days in wet camps. It worked. So we started walking in the rain, exploring the island, which by this time was becoming soggy with water. The soil, a mixture of sand and dirt, was turning to cold mush.

Fortunately the rain let up soon and while there was a cold wind blowing with the let up in the actual downpour we had an opportunity to explore the island, perhaps a mile or more in length and at its widest point a little over a quarter of a mile in width.

There was a period of two or three hours while we waited anxiously for the boats, then we heard the motors approaching and shortly afterwards we all participated in the job of moving things into camp.

That was one of the most disagreeable afternoons I have put in for some time. I carried things back and forth across the muddy soil until I was thoroughly exhausted. I knew that I shouldn't be lifting and carrying those loads. I knew that Murl Emery shouldn't be lifting them. I knew that the girls shouldn't be lifting them. But the stuff was there and we had to get it under cover before dark and it had started to rain again.

With the new load we had additional tents and in our walks we had scared up a little firewood so we got a fire going in the stove. Sam and Pat put up a sleeping tent for the girls and a couple of wigwam tents with floors. Everything was wet and the odor of damp canvas permeated the camp.

We brought out a jug of rum, got some hot water, and had hot buttered rums, then broke out some canned goods and cooked dinner.

Our sleeping bags were wet but, fortunately, had not wet

through, although they gave forth a damp, soggy odor. That night we slept with the sound of rain pelting against the canvas, wind blowing and flapping the tents until it threatened to pull them up by the roots, and always that odor of wet canvas and soggy, down-filled sleeping bags in our nostrils.

I would like to report that, being a nervous individual, I was unable to sleep. Unfortunately, however, the truth of the matter is that I instantly sank into deep slumber and from time to time was only drowsily aware of the pelting rain, the blowing wind, the crashing of surf and the soggy smell.

The next day the storm had temporarily abated and along toward noon the sun came out. We hurriedly dragged wet canvases out and spread them on the ground. We dried out sleeping bags as best we could, moved chairs out into the sunlight and congratulated ourselves that the storm was over.

That night it rained again.

Gradually, however, we managed to get things dried out.

After a person has camped enough in pelting rain there is nothing quite as satisfactory as snuggling into a warm sleeping bag inside of a good tent and listening to the rain beat against the canvas. It gives one a feeling of dry security.

However, all of this wasn't doing our photographic equipment any good. The tents had been pitched on moist ground. The floors of the tents were wet, and no matter what happened we couldn't keep a certain amount of rain from blowing in the openings. Our focal-plane shutters began to stick, the leaves of the between-the-lens shutters started swelling.

Added to this was the effect of hundreds of miles of washboard roads. I know of nothing that will work the devastation to equipment that can be accomplished by a washboarded road unless it is a trotting pack horse in the mountains.

We'd take our tripods and tighten the screws to the last notch. By the time we had gone over a few miles of washboard roads the screws would have been loosened, the tripods would have come to pieces and nuts and bolts would be scattered around the floor of the car. Toothpaste in a bag would jiggle around and the top would come off. Then the pounding of obstacles on the duffel bag would squeeze out the toothpaste all over the clean clothes.

So by the time we got ready to take whale pictures our equipment had already lived through plenty of rough treatment.

Whale hunting turned out to be not as easy as we had anticipated. It was necessary to wait until tidal conditions were right and preferably we needed relatively calm waters. When the wind is blowing riffles there is not much distinction between the appearances of a wind-blown wave twelve inches high and the back of a whale protruding out of water. Also, the light has to be right, and whales somehow have a disconcerting habit of coming up directly between the camera and the sun. When the sun is low on the water this prevents any worth-while picture.

Moreover, there was the irresistible desire to explore some of the surrounding country. So we decided to postpone whale hunting until we had explored the terrain and could count on calm, tranquil waters. But the waters wouldn't get calm. It became apparent that our rain was just a part of a persistent storm, bits of lashing rain and violent squalls interspersed with periods of fitful sunlight.

One day, when the wind was heavy enough to cause something of a turmoil in the water, we went to the mainland directly across from our island camp just for the sake of taking a walk, getting some exercise and exploring.

This was well within the lagoon itself and there were not

supposed to be any really worth-while objects to be found by beachcombing. But we soon found that in the course of time there had been quite a deposit of miscellaneous objects: electric light bulbs which had been discarded from various ships, bits of interesting driftwood and a couple of the glass balls used as floats on fishing nets in the Orient.

Then we turned our attention inland and found several nearly perfect obsidian arrowheads.

It was interesting to note that the coyotes had followed a trail just back of the seashore until they had made a very distinct path.

I presume the coyotes in this area have learned to feed very largely on marine life. Otherwise it is difficult to account for the large number of coyotes around Scammon's Lagoon.

We could hear them every night, and quite frequently during the day we caught sight of them, virtually fearless, maintaining a discreet distance of perhaps a hundred yards or so, but filled with curiosity and pausing from time to time

Driftage—discarded bottles and burned out light bulbs.

to look back over their shoulders as they trotted away, quite frequently turning to stand broadside as they looked us over.

I also suspect that prowling around at night the coyotes get quite a bit of water fowl.

Vast flocks of duck and geese would come winging in along toward evening and settle down in great gatherings within a relatively short distance of the shore.

During the period of maximum activity, when new flocks were coming in, the air would be filled with quackings and honkings, then as darkness approached the birds would huddle together and finally become silent, their heads tucked under their wings, sleeping quietly.

At low tide the waters of the lagoon are very shallow, stretching out in places for perhaps a mile with water only a few inches deep.

Once in the middle of the night when we were camped near where there was a huge raft of geese, we heard the sudden whirr of wings and then literally thousands of birds were flying in panic in the darkness overhead. Their flight was so low and close and their wings beating the air so fast that it sounded something like a jet plane taking off from an airport.

Next morning we found a big pile of feathers and evidences that one or more coyotes had enjoyed a sumptuous repast.

I have an idea that these coyotes have learned to move silently in the shallow water until they can pounce upon some sleeping bird.

After this experience we started looking along the shoreline in the salt water grass and found many a pile of feathers.

The coyotes were well fed—so were we.

One afternoon when we encountered a day which was unfit for whale hunting and we had been exploring the neighboring country, Emery suggested that it might be a good plan to have some fresh fish for supper.

Emery hooks a fish.

We traveled on one motor only, reducing it to trolling speed, and went out around the island where we were camped.

Emery was piloting the boat and Gandara and I were doing the fishing.

We had gone only a few yards when I had a strike and pulled in a nice fish. Gandara dropped his line into the water and within a few seconds had another strike which had his reel buzzing and sent the line hissing through the water. He was using a plug which Emery valued very highly and when, after a few minutes, the fish made off with the plug, I pointed out to Gandara that he hadn't given the fish enough line, that a good fisherman never lost a plug, etc., etc.

After that we both landed several fish, Emery having donated another one of his highly prized bass plugs to the good of the cause.

Then I hooked onto a fish that at first felt like a snag,

Pat, expertly extracting filets from the fish.

then suddenly exploded into action and took off for China. I gave it lots of line and exclaimed that I had hooked a whale.

Then the line went slack. I reeled in and reeled in and reeled in and felt sure I had lost the fish. Then as I was retrieving the last of the slack I found that my line was apparently fouled on something almost directly beneath the boat. I pulled and tugged, putting all the pressure I dared on the line, and nothing happened. I told Emery that I was snagged and he'd have to manipulate the boat so I could recover the plug. Emery started to do this and I was giving a series of little gentle jerks on the line when all of a sudden my fish exploded into activity once more and the reel started smoking. As it slowed down and I was groping for the handle with my thumb and finger to retrieve a little line, and just as I was getting the handle of the reel in my grasp, the fish took off again with such suddenness that he jerked the handle out of my grip, caught my index finger afoul of the reel and for a moment I thought my finger was going to break before I could extricate it.

That gave Mr. Fish all the opportunity he needed. He lunged against the line and snapped it clean in two.

I have seldom seen anyone as pleased as Joe Gandara or as annoyed as Murl Emery.

Gandara pointed out to me from time to time on the way back to our mooring that good fishermen might lose a fish but they seldom lost a plug, etc., etc.

We had some very choice specimens of fish, just a nice pan size of about eighteen to twenty-two inches. Pat expertly extracted fillets from the sides of the fish and that night we had one of the most delicious suppers I have ever tasted.

Mexican corbina caught and cooked all within ninety minutes make a dish that makes my mouth water just thinking back on it.

111

× IX ×

WE CONTACT THE
WHALES

While we were waiting for the sort of weather which would enable us to get good whale pictures we were steadily using up our supplies.

Our supply of fresh water was exceedingly limited. We had to haul it from the mainland and by the time we had our first clear day, in place of hunting whales we had to dash back to the mainland and go to the salt works to replenish our supplies of gasoline and drinking water. There I found frantic messages awaiting me. I must get in touch with Hollywood at once.

Peggy became the sacrificial sheep or, I should say, the goat. We found there was a cargo plane of lobsters which had been forced to make a temporary landing because Ensenada was socked in. It was sitting there with motors running, the pilots on the radio, waiting for word that Ensenada was clear enough to land.

While we were there the pilots got the word all was clear. We negotiated with them to take Peggy, and piled her aboard with the sacks of lobsters to make a rough, dangerous trip to Ensenada where she rented a taxi to take her to Tijuana, another taxi to take her to San Diego, and then telephoned the ranch to have someone come and meet her. She got on the phone with Hollywood and explained to them that she was in there making arrangements for a chartered airplane and that I would be along "at the earliest possible moment."

That gave us a few days to hunt whales, and they were really exciting days.

It soon became apparent that the sound of our powerful motors disturbed the whales and caused them to dive. It *might* have caused them to attack the boats if it weren't for the fact that we were going too fast for the whales to catch up with us, but for the most part the whales simply became frightened.

By this time we had learned enough about whales to know that when a whale submerged and the water became agitated in a series of whirlpools, the whale was getting out of there fast and diving deep all at the same time.

These animals are so powerful that when their huge tails are called on to furnish motive power for a fast dive the water on the surface is churned up into eddies and small whirlpools.

We decided to slow down and try sneaking up on the whales but soon found that didn't work.

So then we decided to go out and anchor the boats, shut off the motors and wait for the whales to come drifting along with the tide.

At the time we didn't realize how risky that could be. We knew that there were certain things which could happen. A whale could get tangled up with the anchor line; or a whale could come to the surface, see us sitting there, decide we were hostile and give us a casual slap with his tail which would put the boat at the bottom and its passengers in the hospital or in a shark's belly.

However, we were still laboring under the delusion that the whales were peaceful so we went out early in the morning and anchored the boats.

The tide changed and soon the whales came drifting along.

The boats were about seventy-five feet apart and sometimes whales would come by one boat, sometimes by another. We felt that colored film would give us a better idea of where the whales began and the water left off, although we knew that for purposes of book publication we would have to limit the pictures to black and white.

So we had cameras with colored film, cameras with black and white film, and movies grinding away on colored film.

I was leaving it up to Sam to take pictures in black and white. I was working a color movie camera with a fairly long focal-length lens.

Over in the other boat Murl and Pat Emery were grinding away with colored movies and Joe Gandara was also taking colored movies. I was the only one who really wanted pictures for publication and I felt that Sam, who is a pretty expert photographer, could be trusted to get good black and white pictures of anything which came along.

Then without previous warning came a moment of terrific excitement. A whale was approaching and unless he changed his course it looked very much as though he were going to pass right between the two boats.

What would he do?

If he came up close to one of the boats, would he ignore it or would he give it a slap with his tail? It was too late to haul up the anchors and start the motors. We had to sit this one out.

Photographers Gandara, Murl and Pat Emery grinding away.

It was amusing to see everyone start putting on life preservers as though someone had given the signal for a boat drill. I know that I was excited and scared, and from the way grown men began to whisper and giggle I gathered the others were sharing at least some of my feelings.

The whale came ploughing majestically on. He passed directly between the boats. I guess he was not over fifteen or twenty feet from us.

I know he was so close that my lens had a problem of parallax with the finder, which I didn't correct, and it wasn't until two-thirds of the whale's length had gone by that I realized what was happening to my pictures. So I elevated the camera in time to get some good pictures of the west end of a whale headed east. Prior to that time my lens was taking some wonderful pictures of the rippling waves thrown up by a huge whale, bigger than a locomotive, ploughing his majestic way through a tranquil sea.

Afterwards it turned out that Sam's camera had given way under the damp air, the rigors of the trip and years of use.

We didn't realize any of this at the time, but were elated at our "close-ups." After this whale passed without paying the slightest attention to us we felt certain we had solved the whale problem and at the same time had a collection of pictures that would be knock-outs.

We had embarked upon this adventure early in the morning before breakfast, and before the girls had crawled out of their sleeping bags. So now we upped anchors and went back to camp. We had a hurried breakfast, picked up the girls, and started out once more and had another adventure—this time with a "baby" whale, which probably had been newly born. He had been injured in some way and the poor thing was looking for his mother. He thought our boats might be Mother, and he started hanging around our boats, swimming in circles and on one occasion actually going under the

A ''baby'' whale at close range.

Gandara, Murl and Pat take close-ups.

boat and coming up underneath it so that the boat slipped off his back.

We got some hurried pictures but the question always arose, where was Mother?

In Mother's eyes this was a poor little destitute offspring in need of attention and protection. To us, he was a seventeen-foot whale still capable of smashing a boat with his tail or upsetting us in the shark-infested waters.

A little of that stuff goes a long way.

We got some photographs which fortunately turned out well and then I suggested to Sam once more that we get the hell out of there.

Then we ran slap-bang into the middle of a whale circus.

I have heard these whale circuses described but no one seems to know exactly what they are.

As nearly as we could determine from this one, one bull whale was making passes at two cows who had young calves with them and who didn't want any part of more romance. The bull whale was swimming in circles, trying to herd the cows into a watery corral. The frightened calves were riding on Mother's backs wherever possible, then jumping completely over Mother and down on the other side.

The whales were so preoccupied with what they were doing that they were completely oblivious to our circling boats.

Here again, however, we had a problem. If we got close enough to get pictures that would be worth anything we were in such dangerous proximity that if one of the whales came up out of the water and rolled over he could roll directly onto one of the boats. If we stayed far enough away with our motors running so that we were out of danger our pictures wouldn't be good.

We started to play it safe but within a short time were circling the churning waters, trying to get pictures.

118

Once more after a few brief passes we broke off the engagement, convinced that we had pictures that would "knock your eye out." I still think I did have, but that particular magazine of movie film was unaccountably lost somewhere in transit. Sam's black and white camera, as it subsequently turned out, was going through the motions of taking pictures without doing any good, and that was that.

However, Joe Gandara got some very good colored movies and fortunately Pat Emery, who is in my opinion one of the best outdoor photographers I have ever encountered, who has made a careful study of photography, who is cool as a cucumber in an emergency, who manages to think of exposure, film speed and all the rest of it at the time when it counts, got some of the most wonderful motion pictures of a whale circus I have ever seen.

Also, as it turned out, Jean, who has become a recent shutterbug convert, secured some very good color shots. Sam's camera unfortunately was the black-and-white mainstay of the expedition at that point.

In dangerous proximity.

× X ×

COMBING A
VIRGIN BEACH

While we had been eager to hunt whales with cameras, we all of us were equally eager to get down to Emery's "virgin" beach.

We made one attempt on a rather windy morning, but soon the wind blew up such a sea that I refused to go all the way and we detoured to shore and then shortly afterwards went back to camp. The wind was blowing hard and the lagoon was a mass of whitecaps. Our boats were heavily loaded with personnel and the Tote Gote and its trailer. We were out there all alone in turbulent waters and I saw no reason to take chances.

The next day the wind had gone down and we loaded the boats and started across. It turned out to be a delightful day and we were able to make a rather uneventful run to the south end of the island where we pulled one of the boats up

Boat loaded with Emery's Tote Gote and trailer.

above the high tideline just in case the weather should change. We anchored the other boat, Emery set up the Tote Gote and trailer and we started combing the beach.

Murl could put two people in the trailer and transport them, so he started out with people in pairs, dropping one off after about a mile, then dropping the other off, then returning for two more.

Gandara elected to stay on the beach photographing whales.

The trouble with this somewhat complicated method of transportation was that it became apparent Emery couldn't possibly explore more than the first three or four miles of the beach and then get everyone back to the boats in time to return to camp before dark.

Driftage of all kinds.

At the time, this didn't seem to be too serious. As always happens on trips of this sort, we were looking forward to future days and were making plans as though we had all the time in the world.

I have seldom enjoyed anything as much as combing the section of beach which had been assigned to me. I found glass balls from the Oriental fish nets; I found driftage of all sorts, wood which had evidently come from China or Japan which still had Oriental characters burnt into the wood. I found an old mooring which had evidently floated around for many years before coming to a final resting place. I found all sorts of bottles, an Oriental shoe which probably hadn't drifted all the way from Japan, although it was of a type not used in this country. It might have gone overboard from a Japanese fishing boat.

There were all sorts of burned out electric lights bulbs of different descriptions, including many discarded radio tubes. There was a broken life ring of the type carried on the decks of steamers to be used in the event of sudden emergencies. And to cap the climax, there was even an old toilet seat deposited on one of the sand hills.

Emery himself had little time for beachcombing. He was running a Tote Gote taxi. But he was tremendously pleased with the performance of the Tote Gote and trailer, and we were planning to come back, make an overnight camp and Emery was going to explore the length and breadth of the beach.

So we went back to our camp on the island filled with many plans and lots of good intentions. However, the next day the weather turned bad again and we decided to go up the lagoon on the sheltered side and explore one of the other islands.

All in all, it was a period of wonderful activity. The excitement of hunting whales, of exploring new territory and the

Emery ferried personal supplies.

thrill of anticipation, looking forward to each new day as ushering in a new adventure. There is nothing that can quite take the place of an experience such as this; a congenial group taking each new adventure as it came.

It soon became apparent, however, that we were pretty much chained down simply by the problem of supplies. We needed to replenish our drinking water cans every two or three days and we couldn't carry enough gasoline in our boats to keep us supplied for more than a couple of days at a time since the distances in the lagoon were so great and since the boats were fed from portable pressure tanks and we only had so many of these tanks.

So whether we wanted to or not, it became necessary to make rather frequent trips over the twenty-odd miles of lagoon to the place where we had left our cars, then drive over the submerged salt pans to the salt works where we could get gasoline and drinking water. Suddenly, and before

Emery's Tote Gote taxi.

we realized it, time was creeping up on us and we still had many things to do. But I knew that I simply had to get in touch with my office by telephone and find out just how much time I had left.

I was hoping I could have another four or five days, but I did have to find out what was going on.

So after we went back to camp we decided to get supplies the next day and I could check up by using the ship-to-shore telephone at the salt works.

Murl Emery is, at heart, an explorer. Someone had told him that if a person was careful in picking channels it was quite possible to take a small boat from Scammon's Lagoon through to Guerrero Negro, by an inside channel that was supposed to connect the two lagoons at high tide.

Emery wanted to try it.

In the meantime, Peggy was back at the ranch collecting scripts, trying to stall off persons who had to see me "right away" and, I knew, trying to cope with all of the emergencies, urgencies and crises which always come up from day to day.

I had told her to line up the different charter airplane outfits so that when I telephoned, if it should appear I was needed, she could have a plane on its way within a matter of minutes.

Emery came up with quite an idea. He would take Jean, Anita, Sam and myself to the mainland with our sleeping bags and all of the camp goods that could be crowded into the two boats, then he would return to the island, would pack up the rest of the camp. He could pilot one boat; Pat could pilot the other. They could take Joe Gandara with them and start out in time to find the channel between Scammon's Lagoon and the Black Warrior Lagoon.

We could go into the salt works, I could telephone the office, and, if necessary, charter a plane and fly in that afternoon and be back the next morning. Murl, Joe and Pat would cross over into the Black Warrior and the next morning around eleven o'clock would be at a designated spot on Black Warrior Lagoon. We could set up a camp there which would be closer to our base of supplies, to drinking water and gasoline, and we could make headquarters there for a day or two. By that time he would have fully charted the channel between the two lagoons and we could go back and forth at will.

By moving camp while I was flying back and forth, we wouldn't lose any time from whale hunting and all I would lose would be a night's sleep.

It sounded like a good idea.

Murl thought he *might* get through to the other lagoon in one day, but he didn't want to take any chances on the tide. He wanted to ride one tide in an unhurried exploration and feel free to camp that night and await the corresponding high tide the next day.

So early in the morning we started breaking camp, and Jean, Anita, Sam and I were put ashore on schedule; which, it must be remembered, was a distance of some twenty or twenty-five miles which we negotiated in heavily laden boats. Then we hurriedly unloaded the stuff and threw it into the cars. Murl and Pat Emery, each at the helm of a boat and fighting to catch the tide, turned on the gas full throttle and went hightailing out of there filled with enthusiasm and with a great waving of hats.

The four of us drove across the submerged salt pans, feeling our way carefully, trying to avoid any possible soft spots, and got into the salt works.

We got a call through to Peggy at the ranch without much difficulty and, sure enough, scripts had piled up, the telephone was ringing, Peggy was stalling everyone as best she could, telling them that I was "expected momentarily." She told me I would simply have to come in to go over some of the television scripts and proofs and handle some of the

127

more urgent matters which had arisen during my absence.

She had a list of all the available charter planes and would have one on its way within a matter of minutes. It would only be necessary for me to call her again to get a confirmation.

So we waited half an hour and called her, only to learn that one of the pilots was down with the Asian flu, another plane which should have been available was in the shop, a third one had been chartered, a fourth which had been leased had been taken on a priority of the owner, and she hadn't found any plane that could make the trip.

In the meantime, she had phoned Hollywood that I would be going over scripts that night and had made several other commitments.

So then from the salt works at Guerrero Negro I started calling airplane companies and so the afternoon wore on.

It had been decided that Sam would accompany me to San Diego while Jean and Anita would stay at the salt works. Peggy had arranged to bring a part of the secretarial staff at the ranch and Sam's wife down to San Diego. They were to leave that afternoon, get suites at the hotel, have typewriters all set up in readiness to start work the minute we arrived.

One of the aviation companies told me it had finally located a Mexican flyer in Tijuana who was available and was on his way. He had in fact left a half hour earlier. I was advised that I could expect him to arrive at about two-thirty.

So we went out and waited.

By three o'clock I began to feel nervous. By three-fifteen I was consulting my watch every few minutes. By three-thirty I was desperate. By three-forty-five I had given him up and was wondering what next to do. Then at four o'clock there was the roar of a motor and a plane swept over the salt works, made a steep bank and circled into the landing field.

Jean, Anita, Sam and I were out there in a matter of

minutes and we met Francisco Munoz, a veteran Mexican pilot with whom we were destined to become much better acquainted in the weeks that followed.

Since it got dark a little after five o'clock, I felt certain that Munoz would insist on waiting overnight, so I asked him hopelessly, and simply as a matter of routine, if he could get us to Tijuana that night.

Munoz is a short, stocky, volatile individual packed with energy and optimism.

"Oh, seguro! Sure, sure, sure! Most certainly. Get in, get in!"

So Sam and I crawled into the plane.

Jean insisted I should take an overcoat. The radio had said there was an intensely cold spell gripping Southern California.

I vetoed the suggestion. The plane would be warm and after we landed at Tijuana it would be only a short ride to San Diego.

There wasn't time for any protracted argument. Munoz literally hurled the plane down the runway and up into the air and we were off.

After we had become fairly well settled I looked at my watch, did some hasty mental arithmetic and said, "How are you going to get to Tijuana by dark?"

"Oh, not by dark," he said. "But tonight, sure."

"How long?" I asked.

"Two hours and seventeen minutes from now," he said optimistically.

I glanced at my watch and did mental arithmetic again. That was going to get us in around six-thirty-five. It would have been good and dark for at least an hour and we would have been flying in a single-motored plane over rugged terrain where emergency landing fields are virtually nil.

However, we were up in the air and there was nothing to

129

do but settle back, make myself comfortable, and enjoy the flight.

Munoz had the plane in a steep climb and it wasn't long before we were skimming along at about ten thousand feet.

At that elevation the chill was penetrating.

I asked him about the heater.

Munoz took both hands off the wheel to make a characteristic gesture.

"Is broken," he said.

So I settled back to a tooth-chattering journey through the late afternoon sunlight, early dusk and then Stygian darkness, cussing myself for not having taken the overcoat.

I don't know yet why the tail assembly of that plane didn't crystallize and drop off. I was shivering so hard the entire back of the plane must have been shaking like an electric razor gone mad.

We finally saw the lights of Ensenada and, shortly after that, Tijuana. A little before eight-thirty Sam and I came walking in to the U. S. Grant Hotel in San Diego, probably two of the most disreputable-looking characters who had ever entered the place; clad in clothes which had been splashed with salt spray, soaked with rain water, spotted with oil and, I am ashamed to confess, probably with syrup from pancakes and an occasional drip of bacon grease.

We hadn't shaved since we had left the ranch. I had needed a haircut when I left but hadn't had time to get one during the holiday season, and it is safe to say that I was even more in need of a haircut by the time I pushed my way up to the desk and encountered the steely eyes of the clerk.

However, the girls had already arranged for suites of rooms, had set up their typewriters and were ready for work, and as soon as the hotel employees identified us they were cordiality itself.

I took the elevator to the room the girls had fixed up as an office and was dismayed to see the size of the pile of stuff that was stacked up.

I didn't dare leave the room. I couldn't take time to shave or even clean up. There was a pile of scripts to be gone over. I sent the rest of the party out to dinner, had a thick steak sent up to the room and sat there pouring words into my faithful dictating machine between bites of steak.

My secretaries came back after dinner, took the records into another suite and started typing.

That night was something of a nightmare. Files of urgent correspondence were stacked up, scripts were piled one on top of the other. It was around three o'clock in the morning when I finally got into a hot bath and got the whiskers off my face.

I was up by daylight and the girls drove us down to the border where we were to meet Munoz. There had been no time for a haircut. I kept dictating all the way in the automobile.

Munoz met us right on schedule. We crossed the border, adjusted the seat belts in his plane and by noon we were approaching Guerrero Negro.

One of the reasons we had been in such a hurry was to time things so that by the time the Emerys and Joe Gandara arrived at the new campsite we would be there to meet them.

The afternoon before, while we had been waiting for the plane, we had driven one of the jeeps to the new camp-site and left it there with the key in the ignition and a note telling them we were taking a plane and suggesting that if they arrived before we did they could drive up to the salt works.

So we suggested to Munoz as we approached Guerrero Negro that he swing around by the new campsite and we could see whether the boats were there and the car was gone, or whether the boats were there and the new camp had been set up.

As we circled the place it became apparent that the car was right where we had left it the afternoon before, the boats were not there, and there was no sign of the boats in Guerrero Negro Lagoon.

So we asked Munoz to circle the lagoon, then fly over the connecting channels between Scammon's Lagoon and Guerrero Negro and then, just to give us a good view of things, we could fly over the island beach and give it a good once-over.

We soon located the boats. They were out in the vast series of sandy mud flats separating the two lagoons. From the air these sandy mud flats seemed to be quite extensive.

We could only surmise that there had been a dispute over the location of the channel because Pat had gone on one side of an island and was hard aground, and Emery had gone on the other side and was hard aground. They were both out of the boats and wading in an attempt to find a channel.

From the air it seemed absurdly easy to differentiate between the channels which wound among the flats of sand and mud, but we knew that from down on the water where the boats were located it was a virtual impossibility to tell where the channels were.

One thing was certain: The boats were never going to get to the Guerrero Negro Lagoon early that afternoon, and from my observations I felt they couldn't make it at all.

However, we dipped low over the boats and wagged our wings reassuringly, waved encouragement, and then flew out over Scammon's Lagoon to look at the whales and then make a pass over the virgin beach.

A whale seen from the air presents a very remarkable spectacle. It looks like a submarine lying just below the surface of the water, or coming up to spout a cloud of white vapor.

Mother whales lay just below the surface of the water while the baby whales reposed just above them or perhaps just a little to one side.

As we flew over the lagoon great flocks of geese arose below us and we were looking at the whales through white clouds of wild fowl.

Then we made a swing over the virgin beach and I am ashamed to say that I missed it entirely. I became very much disappointed in what I saw. As it turned out, I was looking far too close to the shoreline and wasn't looking back far enough in the low sand hills where the wreckage had been deposited during periods of storm and high tide. On later air trips I corrected this mistake, but at the time I derived an erroneous impression. All I can say by way of explanation is that it takes quite a bit of practice to appraise a beach from a speeding airplane.

If the plane is too high, the objects one wishes to observe are flattened out to nothing. If one flies too low, the skimming sand whizzes by faster than the eye can appraise it.

Anyhow, I muffed it. I came to the conclusion that while this beach was fascinating, the rest of the unexplored sandy stretch wasn't greatly different from the four miles we had already explored.

In the light of subsequent developments my face was destined to become very red indeed.

On the way back we made one more survey of the channels and even allowing for the fact that the tide was a long ways from full, I still felt that the boats couldn't make it.

Munoz said that on his way back to Tijuana he could drop a message which the boatmen would receive. So we landed at the salt works, transported ourselves to a building which the management had very generously placed at our disposal, and I wrote a note to the boats telling them to go back to the first camp on Scammon's Lagoon.

Gandara had one favorite story which he told from time to time about the stranger asking the native how to get to the post office. The man had said, "Well, let's see. You go two blocks straight ahead, then turn to the left three blocks . . . no, that road's torn up. I tell you what you'd better do. You'd better go to the left for four blocks, then turn to the right for two blocks . . . no, that road hasn't been cut through." The man paused and thought for a moment, then slowly shook his head. "I'm sorry," he said. "You can't get to the post office from here."

So I wrote a note in which I referred to the Emerys as "landlubbers" which I knew would raise their blood pressure sufficiently to make up for any lack of hot coffee, told them they couldn't get to the post office from there, and to come home. Sam took the note to Munoz to deliver, but while he was waiting for Munoz to take off, found one of the local residents who scoffed at the idea that the Emerys couldn't get through. They simply had blundered on to the wrong channel. There was, he explained, one of the men at the salt works who knew every foot of the lagoon and could get them through on the evening tide without the slightest question of doubt. He would arrange to have that man leave at once in a boat, hunt up the stranded boatmen, show them the right channel, and they would be in shortly after dark.

So Sam, prompted by optimism, tore up my note and hurriedly scribbled another note reading, "Stay where you are. A professional pilot is on his way to guide you landlubbers to safety. Wait for him."

Munoz took off with a roar of the motor and with rare skill managed to drop the note almost exactly into Emery's upthrust hands; quite a feat when one considers wind and velocity.

Emery waved his acknowledgment, Munoz dipped his wings and headed back for Tijuana.

The pilot duly went out and found that the high tide was unusually low, that the channel he had expected to use couldn't be navigated, and so turned back.

We waited all night for the Emerys to join us, rolling into our sleeping bags when it became apparent they had missed the afternoon high tide and couldn't possibly arrive until the next day.

The next day we talked with the man who had taken the boat down in an attempt to reach the channel and he felt that it was impossible for the boats to make the grade with tides such as we were having at the moment. But in any event, the high, high tide came late at night; the high tide during the afternoon was not high enough to get the boats through, even with the aid of pushing and dragging.

It happened that the executive airplane used by the salt works was on the strip at the moment and Mr. McClaughry suggested that if we wanted to make another survey of the situation, the pilot would be glad to take us out over the lagoon.

By this time we were getting somewhat worried. The party had been out for two nights and along the water the nights can become exceedingly damp.

It was apparent that the boats had been very heavily loaded and were not only drawing a lot of water, but that it would have been difficult for the boatmen to unpack sleeping bags and camp stuff.

So we got in the plane and made a swing out over the stranded boats.

We found that the two Emerys had waded ashore, leaving Gandara in the boats and it was a rather bedraggled-looking Gandara who waved at us as we went overhead.

So we made a circle and came on the two Emerys far out ahead of the boats, exploring the channels at low tide. From the distance which separated them from the boats, they must have been walking since daylight. This time I scribbled a note giving them the figures of tide elevation for that particular point and advised them, "You can't get to the post office

135

from here. Go back to the first camp at Scammon's Lagoon and we will meet you there."

We flew low over the Emerys to drop the note and as they saw the plane gliding down toward them until it was only a few feet off the ground, Pat Emery, in a joking gesture, dropped to his knees and elevated his hands as though to push the plane back into the air. We dropped a note and then circled and came back over them to make sure they had it. Later on I assured Pat Emery I had photographed him while he was down on his knees with arms upraised, thanking a merciful heaven for having sent us to the rescue and that this photograph, properly captioned, would be released to the press on our return. Pat couldn't tell from my dead pan expression whether I was ribbing him or not. For a while, since I insisted Sam and I be treated as rescuing heroes and kept speculating on whether we would receive medals, I had him worried.

The company pilot, "Mike," (Miguel Angel Marquez) a remarkably skillful pilot, had dropped the note within only a few feet of the Emerys and they waved their hands and the note, signifying that they had it and were in accord with my suggestion.

So we once more circled over the boats to wave reassuringly to Gandara. We noticed that each boat was equipped with a long mast-like pole to the top of which had been tied a red bandana. We found out afterwards that this was so they wouldn't lose each other in the twisting channels as they went through the sand hills, and would enable the one boat to follow the other. (At the time I was somewhat concerned lest it was a signal of distress.)

Everyone seemed in good health so we returned to the landing strip and Jean, Anita, Sam and I loaded up the cars and again drove back over the submerged salt pans to the place where we had made our first camp.

We felt that the boatmen would have a good thirty miles of travel but could make it in less than two hours. So, with the aid of binoculars, we started looking for them. It wasn't until nearly three o'clock in the afternoon, however, that we first sighted them limping in.

As they came close to the landing we saw that the boats were really too heavily loaded and were, as a result, drawing much more water than they should have. In fact, they even ran aground in negotiating the channel to the campsite.

We found out afterwards that we only knew a small part of it. The boats had been so loaded that it had been hard to manipulate the steering gear by means of the rope which stretched from the steering wheels in front to the motors behind. Because there were two motors on each boat, the rope was pulling on a short leverage and the heavy load put considerable strain on the ropes. They had given way time after time in attempting to swing the heavily loaded boats around short turns. The boatmen had spliced and tied until they had no more slack left for repairs.

I suggested to Emery that maybe we could go back down to the south end of the island and explore the "virgin beach" by Tote Gote.

I have never seen people who were less enthusiastic about starting back down Scammon's Lagoon with heavily loaded boats.

It turned out they had had a most uncomfortable night. They hadn't been able to get ashore for fear of having the boats left high and dry when the tide changed. They had therefore tried to sleep in the boats and the damp chill had penetrated their bones. They had spent two cramped nights in the channel and they were not keen about starting out on another thirty-five mile trip.

Yet, if we were going to make a camp on the south end of the island we would have to start at once with the two loaded boats, split up the camp and wait until the next day to make another trip with the second boat load. The boats were out of gasoline and would have to be refilled from our reserve supplies, and it would probably take us all the next day to get established on the island. Since it looked as though the next day might be windy, the problem of taking heavily loaded boats thirty-five miles through a windblown chop was not too inviting.

"We can't make it this trip," I said. "That beach is going to have to wait."

Murl and Pat exchanged glances. "Let's go home," Pat said.

Murl said, "Okay. We've got our whale photographs, most of the stuff we want. We've done a bit of exploring. We have a good five days of rough roads ahead of us, even if we have the best luck in the world. If there should be another rain storm we'll be marooned in mud around Punta Prieta. It looks as though there is another storm coming and our best bet is to try to beat this storm and get past Punta Prieta while the roads are still passable."

So we decided to unload the boats, put them on the trailers, make an overnight camp and leave as early as possible the next morning.

× XI ×

TROUBLE

It was on the trip home that the mechanical gremlins began to catch up with us.

Veterans who knew the country and who had seen us embarking with two nineteen-foot boats in tow had shaken their heads glumly and decided that the boats would necessarily be left by the side of the road somewhere and we'd be lucky if we didn't have to leave the cars as well and try to walk out.

The first mechanical casualty was one of the gearshifts. Some connecting hootenanny, (Sam says it was something in the clutch linkage) which I know nothing about (as a mechanic I'm a total loss; I can't tell the front end of a spark plug from a rear differential) crystallized and gave way. We couldn't shift gears and the road was too rough to tow the car.

Emery's trailer hitch gives way . . . and is repaired.

Emery crawled under the car, took a look, crawled out, got up to his tool box, pulled out a long tent spike, tossed it down to Pat and said, "Fix it."

Pat got out a gasoline torch and a hammer. He and Sam improvised a blacksmithing forge. They heated the metal red-hot and shaped it. They took a portable drill and drilled it until the drill broke. Then they took the stub of the broken drill and shaped it with a file so that they made another drill out of it and continued drilling.

By nine o'clock that night they had the car fixed and it worked. Moreover, it was such a nice job of part construction that after I got the car into a garage when we got home the man looked at it, shook his head and said, "I can't improve on that. It's just as good as the original part."

The next casualty was Emery's trailer hitch. Because he had lots of room in the boat, there was a temptation to keep piling things in it until finally the metal in his trailer hitch crystallized and gave way and there we were with a nineteen-foot boat and a terrific load of material in it and no trailer hitch. We were still four hard days from the border.

The two Emerys and Sam went to work. They rigged up various and sundry expedients, some of which worked for a few miles, some of which worked longer. Then finally they virtually discarded the trailer hitch altogether. They hammered two pieces of wood into the side supports of the pick-up, they wrapped a chain around and around these supports and down to the trailer, then they put on a "come-along" and tightened the whole thing in such a way that the chain became as taut as a violin string.

It held firmly all the way to the border.

It wasn't until after we had returned and had taken stock of the situation that I realized the extent to which we had failed in our objectives.

One magazine of my colored films had been lost in transit.

141

Where there should have been seven, there were only six. An investigation showed this was the most important fifty feet of all my pictures and it will be remembered that Sam's camera had developed a light leak and shutter trouble as well. All of his pictures had a slight fogging, and those which were taken toward the light were ruined, and that included the film of the whale which had been within some fifteen feet of our boat.

Murl Emery had set up his Tote Gote and trailer on the south end of the beach he had wanted to explore but had been so courteous that he had first given everybody a preliminary ride. The girls had found so many of the glass balls that they had gone wild and Emery had spent the only day he had on the beach acting virtually as a Tote Gote taxi driver. We had expected to get back for another trip but weather conditions and business exigencies had prevented.

Despite the fact we had been away more than three weeks, that my desk was piled high with emergency matters and all of my business associates were hoping that I now had Baja California "out of my system" and would stay home, I decided we were going back.

My friend, Mahlon Vail, one of the owners of the ninety-six thousand acre cattle ranch which adjoins my property, offered to put all of our stuff aboard a big cattle boat which the company uses to ship cattle back and forth from Santa Rosa Island to the mainland.

Don Douglas, who has always been fascinated by Scammon's Lagoon and the whales, invited me to come in and look at the motion pictures they had taken on the second expedition, an expedition about which I had known nothing.

This was the expedition that had used helicopters instead of boats in an attempt to get the heartbeat of the whale. It had the co-operation of the Mexican Government, the United States Army and the National Geographic Society. Everything which could have been done by the aid of modern equipment and modern science was done. No expense was spared, no effort was spared. Moreover, a thoroughly professional job of filming had been done, and Douglas suggested Vail and I could have lunch with him and view the pictures at that time.

Gandara, in the meantime, had gone down to Ensenada, had contacted some of our mutual friends there, had gone to Mexicali, had conferred with the Governor and the executive officers of Baja California and found that there was a widespread interest in our expedition.

Several of the prominent businessmen of Ensenada had become annoyed that all of the publicity about Baja California seemed to settle on vice conditions in Tijuana. No one seemed to know anything about the country around Ensenada, about the country to the south, or about the type of solid, substantial citizens who represent the core of Baja California business and industry. These businessmen pledged themselves to do anything within reason that we wanted.

Almost overnight it seemed that everyone wanted to cooperate.

At the lunch with Mahlon Vail and Donald Douglas, Douglas showed us a superb film which had the best whale pictures anyone could possibly obtain. These pictures, taken from helicopters, showed the manner in which the whales swam through the water, the manner in which they used tails and flippers. Taken from above, the color demarcation between whale and water was sharply defined and the pictures represented a thoroughly professional job.

Gandara, attending a meeting of citizens in Ensenada, wired that all sorts of co-operation was in readiness and that he wanted to go back.

So almost as soon as we returned we were organizing another expedition for Scammon's Lagoon.

It turned out insurance difficulties in connection with the Vail cattle boat would delay us five or six days, and there was some question whether the boat drew too much water to get across the dangerous bar at the lagoon. For a while we contemplated going by air, then decided to load our equipment and retrace our steps by automobile.

Gandara reported that his friend in Ensenada, head of one of the big fishing companies with boats scattered from Ensenada to Cedros Island, had sent wireless instructions to the captain of one of his boats requesting him to have the boat tied up at the wharf at Guerrero Negro Saturday morning, to await our arrival and to put the boat completely at our disposal.

All we had to do was to get to Guerrero Negro by Saturday morning.

This time we didn't take any trailers. I had purchased a Land Rover and we loaded up our cars and made time over the road. We were at Guerrero Negro Saturday morning. We loaded our gear on the fishing boat and arranged for a take-off bright and early Sunday morning.

It seemed that everyone wanted to co-operate. The salt company placed its best pilot at our disposal. This man, Enrique Romero, knows every foot of water in the lagoons and along the coast. The captain of the boat, Fernando Moreno, a veteran, careful, methodical seaman, quietly competent, knew exactly what could be done and what couldn't be done. I never saw him the least excited during the entire trip. I never saw him when he wasn't watchful, alert and completely on the job.

He was accompanied by his son, Fernando, and a Mexican seaman, Augustin Ortiz, whom we nicknamed "Mucho Ojo," because of his enthusiasm for the venture, the manner in which he would stand watch for whales and his uncanny ability to see everything everywhere. That man had the most wonderful pair of eyes. He could see a whale surface, and then from the top of the mast could tell which direction under water he was going and follow him.

We took along Emery's Tote Gote, and this time we decreed that Emery wasn't going to be courteous to anyone. He had bought that Tote Gote to explore the virgin beach on the island, and, by George, he was going to explore it. He wasn't going to give anyone a ride and he was going to comb every one of those miles of virgin beach without trying to be generous.

The trip by water from Guerrero Negro to Scammon's Lagoon is quite an adventure in itself. One must follow a rather tricky channel out of Guerrero Negro until reaching the open sea, then turn abruptly and, after some twenty miles of water which can be very rough indeed, cross inside a bar in a channel that is marked only by natural landmarks and can be located only by good seamanship. The boat has to go within a stone's throw of raging, roaring breakers that pile up into huge waves, dash across shoals with the speed of an express train and then curl over in crashing spray on the shallows. To make any miscalculation and be caught in those shallows is certain disaster.

However, we had a delightful trip, and entering the lagoon came to anchor at the south end of the island Emery wanted to explore. We dropped the anchor in deep water within a hundred yards of the shore and started unloading.

Because we had brought no trailers on this trip, I had suggested to Sam that we should keep our supplies at a minimum. Quite naturally I had been pouring words into a dictating machine while Sam and Emery had been packing. I didn't realize until we arrived and started unpacking the extent to which they had followed my instructions and what they meant by a minimum.

We had one tent as a place in which to eat and store

The author dictating while camp gear is being unloaded.

Our camp outfit piled on the beach.

camera equipment in case of inclement weather. We had a couple of "tarps" and that was all our shelter.

But we made a hurried camp and then went to work. Emery started out on his Tote Gote and Gandara and I climbed up to the upper pilothouse on the boat.

It had been Gandara's theory that much of our photographic trouble had been because we were too close to the water. He felt that if we could get more elevation and whales could come close to us, we could get some good pictures.

I subscribed to this theory, but after seeing the pictures taken by the Douglas expedition from helicopters, I felt that the mast of a boat might not be high enough unless we could get the whales to come very close to the boat.

There was one type of picture which we wanted to get as close to the water as possible, and for that reason Emery had brought along his rubber raft and we had brought an outboard motor.

These pictures were pictures of whales jumping and standing on their tails.

I don't know how a whale stands on his tail, but he does it. Apparently he only does it when he wants to look around, and he prefers to do it during calm weather.

On our previous trip, while we were camped on the island, we would look out, usually in the early morning and, at a distance of a mile or so, see whales come up out of the water to stand on their tails. By using binoculars and telescopes we could get a pretty good idea of the procedure. The whale would thrust his head out of the water for ten or twelve feet, then very slowly, and presumably balanced on his tail, thrust up another ten feet or so of his body until he would apparently be standing some twenty feet above the water. He would stand there for what seemed to be four or five seconds, then would slowly submerge, and at such times there would be no splash.

On the other hand, we had seen whales coming up out of the water at great speed, extending their flippers and then lunging downward with a splash that sent water up in the air for what seemed to be a height of thirty or forty feet.

Our friend, Justo, the turtle hunter, told us that at such times the whales were trying to protect their young and were frightening away sharks.

Whether his idea was true or not, it certainly seemed that these were aggressive tactics on the part of whales and were resorted to for some very definite reason.

There was still a third maneuver which whales made: they would apparently travel at top speed, then come up straight out of the water, not standing on their tails; then they would take a good look around and lunge forward.

We didn't have any pictures showing these activities and the question of whether whales fed or not while they were in southern waters was still a matter of debate. We had seen whales engaged in maneuvers which we thought were associated with feeding, but we couldn't be sure.

At times when the tides would change, we would see whales congregating in the eddies where the tides meet. They would swim around in circles and give every appearance of feeding, but we couldn't see under the water and all we could see were occasional fins, parts of tails or a brief glimpse of a back and the dipping circle where whales came up, spouted and went down again.

All the time we were learning more and more about whales.

Enrique was still scarred from an experience he had had only a few days previously. He had taken two men out to paint a buoy, one of the big steel channel markers anchored beside the channel and used to guide ships into Guerrero Negro.

Enrique was sitting in the boat. The other two men, by means of ropes, had climbed up to the top of the buoy.

Suddenly two whales appeared close by. One of them thrust his head up in order to take a good look, then both of them made for the boat.

Enrique stood his ground.

One of the whales punched the boat with his nose, then the other one came up and nuzzled it. That was too much for Enrique.

He grabbed a rope and scampered up the side of the buoy. He had not been particularly choosy about the method of ascent. He just wanted to get up there fast. He still had evidences of the deep scratches on his legs where he had scraped them in his climb.

The two whales hung around and held the men up on that buoy for nearly an hour. They seemed to enjoy having their quarry treed. From time to time they would stand up on their tails in the water to look at the men from a level stance, then they would go down and swim around the buoy, then they would come up and nuzzle the boat. Then they would swim off and, like cats playing with a mouse, pretend to be disinterested, only suddenly to return.

Enrique had never had anything like that happen before in the eleven years he had been around the lagoons.

It was his idea that whales were absolutely and completely unpredictable, that each whale was a law unto himself and that any whale could attack any boat at any time, although he felt certain the majority of whales were inclined to be peaceful.

Following my instructions, Peggy on her return had ordered every book she could find on whales, and in the brief reading I had done after I returned I found that the authorities seemed to agree the gray whale was quite unpredictable, that during the mating season the bulls were very apt to charge a boat, that quite frequently baby whales would become confused and think a boat was Mother and would start circling. At such times, the real mother would very probably want the boat out of there and would stage tactics designed to accomplish that purpose.

The truth of the matter was that no one knew very much about gray whales because, from the time the commercial whalers abandoned Scammon's Lagoon up until a few short years ago, the gray whale had been presumed to be virtually extinct. Then it had started returning in numbers to Scammon's Lagoon. However, aside from the expeditions by The Scripps Institution of Oceanography and by Don Douglas, little was known about them.

Don Douglas certainly had a wholesome respect for whales. Having been in that boat and experienced the impact of a whale's tail, then having watched the whale turn and charge, smashing the strong sides of a well-constructed boat into kindling wood, Douglas didn't have to read about whales in books. He knew about them. He had been there. No one could tell him a whale wouldn't attack. He had been on the receiving end.

It followed therefore that we realized we had been pretty lucky on our first expedition not to have had a physical encounter with an angry whale and therefore we made certain rules for our safety. One, we wouldn't go out in any of the small boats without life preservers and without having the big boat standing by for rescue in case of attack. Two, we wouldn't go out in the rubber raft at all unless a rescue boat was standing by. Three, we wouldn't get out in the whale channels without having our life preservers put on and securely fastened.

As far as the big boat was concerned, despite the fact that whales had been known to attack the whaling ships, we felt we were perfectly safe.

So having made these rules, and since Emery was more interested in beachcombing than in whales at that time, and while some of the others were making camp, while Emery was starting up the beach on his Tote Gote to satisfy the burning curiosity which had been eating him for some three years, Gandara and I took our stations on the rocking, heaving platform of the fishing boat, cocked our shutters and settled down to wait.

Here again we found that the whales had a couple of trumps we knew nothing about.

It takes rather a long focal-length lens to get an image of a whale that is big enough to enlarge properly. As before mentioned, a long focal-length lens requires a firm, steady foundation.

Just in order to show us that getting whale photographs wasn't a simple matter, windstorms came up which kept the boat rocking and swaying, and from our platform high above the deck, the rocking was so accentuated that it was impossible to find a firm camera platform.

We compensated for this as far as possible by speeding up our shutters, but while we were seated waiting for whales to show up, we would gradually accustom ourselves to the rolling and pitching of the boat. Then, when a whale would show up and we would jump to our feet, it would always take us several seconds to get our balance and brace ourselves against the rail or hang onto a rope in such a way that we could sight our cameras.

Several times I jumped to my feet, elevated my camera, and just as I was snapping the shutter, the motion of the boat would throw me off balance so that my picture turned out to be a picture of the rail of the boat or the ocean directly below the boat or a good cross-section of sky.

Moreover, when it came to jumping whales, the whale knew when he was going to jump. No one else did. It turned out that the action is much faster than a person would believe, and from the time a whale starts to jump until he is back in the water consumes only a very small amount of time. Getting a camera into action, pointed in the right direction and held steady enough to give a sharp image is quite a problem.

We saw lots of whales. We saw lots of jumping whales. We saw whales that were close by. We saw whales that were in the distance. Strangely enough, however, we saw very few whales standing on their tails on this trip and those that we saw were quite some distance away.

Once, when we left camp and took the boat out a mile or so away in order to explore a new channel, we looked back and saw a whale come up right where the boat had been and stand on his tail, looking at Emery.

All we could do was to watch through powerful binoculars.

Emery, who had been exploring the beach on his Tote Gote, had just returned and didn't have a camera available. We could see him watch the whale and the whale watch Emery. It seemed that the whale was a good twenty feet out of the water and Emery said he felt the whale was standing at least that high.

As above mentioned, whales are utterly unpredictable.

However, we did have some luck.

Whales began to get accustomed to the boat. They would move by the anchored boat without paying any attention to it after we had been anchored there for a couple of days.

As whales began to take the boat for granted it was only natural that we began to take the whales for granted. And this lulled us into a false sense of security, which is about the only way I can account for the situation in which we subsequently found ourselves.

On one occasion, Gandara and I saw that two whales were going to swim between the boat and the shore. We alerted the party on shore and they all ran out with cameras.

It was an awe-inspiring sight to see these two huge mam-

Emery up to his knees taking pictures.

mals swimming calmly and complacently between Emery, who had waded out up to his knees in order to take a picture from the shore. Gandara and I were standing on the upper deck of the anchored boat, shooting down.

I hoped Gandara's colored pictures were good. I was shooting black and white and the lead whale submerged just as I was about to take the picture. I had to swing the camera to take a picture of the second whale.

Looking down from this height, the black sides of the whale and the blue of the water mingled together so that the picture contains little suggestion of the thrill of excitement that accompanied the passing of the whales.

On shore, Sam got a very good picture showing the whales passing close to the boat. But, here again, he was handicapped by the fact that only some twelve or eighteen inches of the whale is out of water when he comes up to blow while he is swimming along. And on black and white film the result is singularly unimpressive.

Enrique, Sam and I decided to try out the rubber raft, so we got it inflated and then found that in shipment the transom to which the outboard motor was attached had split in two.

Emery dragged in a piece of driftwood and by use of a hand ax, ingenuity and the co-operation of the Mexican crew of the boat, manufactured a rough-and-ready transom which seemed to do the job.

So that afternoon, as soon as the new transom had been put in place and the motor attached, Enrique and Sam wanted to try it out and I decided to go along just to see how the raft would work with a full load. Sam picked up his camera and on that trip I was literally wearing my cameras so, as it happened, we had them with us, but nothing was farther from our minds than going out into whale territory or trying to take photographs. We didn't even have our life preservers. I certainly thought we were going to be cruising between the shore and the anchored boat and I doubt if anyone else had any different ideas.

The bay was calm. The sun was shining and, as it turned out, the motor was purring gently, smoothly propelling the raft at a speed which seemed to me to be around five or six miles an hour. Sam was adjusting the motor so in place of cruising in a circle we kept the rubber raft pointed straight in order to give him a better chance to make the adjustment.

Because we were all concentrating on the motor and the raft, we got farther from shore and farther from the boat than we had intended. Then suddenly we saw a great commotion in the water about half a mile away. There were huge splashes, great surging black bodies seething and writhing in the water. Clouds of spray were flung up to heights that seemed to be twenty or thirty feet. Occasionally veritable geysers of water would seem to erupt.

Promptly we forgot all about our rules, about the fact that we had no life preservers, no supporting boat, absolutely no safety factor.

We simply wanted to get closer to have a look—and go closer we did.

The party on shore were watching us with binoculars, waiting for us to turn back, ready to heave up the anchor on the fishing boat and start after us if we got into trouble. They realized what we didn't take into account in our excitement. If the whales sensed our presence and resented it, we were completely helpless in that rubber raft. It wouldn't have taken a charge by a whale to have upset us—just a nudge with a nose or a slap with a tail and we would have been struggling in the water, a tempting meal for any shark that was hanging around.

If, on the other hand, the whales didn't resent us or were completely oblivious of our presence, if the vortex of activity should shift our way no rubber raft could hope to last in the midst of a maelstrom such as that; and certainly no one-hundred-seventy-pound individual could survive having a thirty-ton whale drop down on him from a height of ten or fifteen feet.

As we afterwards discovered, the people on shore never expected we were trying to get really close to any such dangerous activity as that. They knew that it would be some fifteen minutes before the men on the big boat could have raised its anchor, got the engines started and reached us, and they assumed we were going to turn back to safety.

Aboard the raft we had long since quit thinking about rules or the safety factor. We couldn't understand what was causing all this surging and splashing, and human curiosity being what it is, and the zeal of the hunter being what it is, we simply felt we had to get closer so we could see whatever was happening. By the time we got close enough to see what was happening the whole melee swung in our direction and approached us at a bewildering speed. Then the activity veered slightly to one side and again remained stationary.

Sam, so engrossed in hunting that nothing else mattered, shut off the motor and Enrique held the boat in position by using the rubber paddle.

By that time we were close enough to see what it was all about and the minute I found out what it was I became acutely aware of our position.

Three bull whales and an acquiescent, amorous female of the species were engaged in a series of maneuvers which apparently included a battle among the bulls and coy encouragement on the part of the cow.

I started taking pictures because there was nothing else to do but I felt my enthusiasm draining out of my toes. We couldn't start the motor in time to do any good. Even if we had the motor running at full speed we couldn't get that raft away from there in time to do any good.

The rapidity with which the whale vortex of activity had shifted toward us had been sufficient proof of that.

The whales were so intent upon what they were doing they paid absolutely no attention to us, and in that there was an element of danger because if they came only a few feet closer we were apt to be squeezed to a pulp. If, on the other hand, one of the whales resented our being there the situation was just as bad.

By this time it became very apparent even to a casual ob-

As we approach the whales Enrique uses sign language.

server that the whales were in that condition which can best be described as being "emotionally aroused."

Enrique, I think, was as excited as we were and kept protesting that this was a phase of whale activity which had never before been witnessed, either by him or by anyone he knew, and Enrique had spent eleven years in the lagoons.

Apparently one of the male whales would get in complete readiness to consummate his conquest of the acquiescent cow, when another bull, getting under him and charging with all of his might, would throw the first bull out of the way and up into the air. The displaced bull, quite apparently all in readiness for what was to have been an amorous interlude, found himself pushed high into the air and rolled over on his back. He would therefore return in angry indignation to find

Whales emotionally aroused.

that the bull who had supplanted him was in turn being shouldered out by a third bull.

As to whether any of the huge mammals were successful in their conquest is still an open question. These things were happening too fast for anyone to keep track of what was going on. There was a great splashing. Great clouds of spray and intertwined whale bodies would engage in water-thrashing activities; then one would shoot up into the air and come down with a terrific splash.

The agitation of the water threw our rubber raft into violent motion. It was almost impossible to hold a camera steady. However, Sam got one memorable picture showing a displaced bull while being rolled over on his back at a most inconvenient time—for the whale. This picture was

sharp enough to stand enlargement, despite the way in which the raft was being thrown around by the waves resulting from the violent activity.

I was whirring away with my motion picture camera and, as it turned out, have some forty feet of colored film showing an activity which may never before have been photographed.

Those who were watching us from the shore with binoculars saw that we were so close to what was taking place that they thought we were right in the midst of a veritable maelstrom of whales, of plunging bodies, smashing tails and surging waters. They started shouting frantically to the fishing boat to get the anchor up and get under way. Through the binoculars it seemed that the raft had become disabled and was right in the midst of a melee of charging whales.

However, before the boat could get the anchor up the whole surging activity suddenly went into lateral motion again and this time, fortunately, it was away from the rubber raft. The instincts of a hunter being what they are, Sam jerked the starting cord of the motor, attempting to follow; and then suddenly as the motor churned into action, we glanced back toward the shore and were surprised to find how small the fishing boat seemed in the distance.

Rather sheepishly we exchanged glances as we all three simultaneously thought of the rules we had made.

And then, as suddenly as it had started, the commotion of whales subsided and the water became calm. Our plunging whales had simply disappeared.

I don't know how the others felt but I know my knees were shaking with excitement. I had a hard time getting my voice to work but I pointed to the shore and finally said, "Sam, let's get the hell out of here."

That remark turned the trick. Three rather scared but excited individuals poured the gas into the motor and that rubber boat started back to camp.

On shore some of the party were watching us through binoculars and others were gesticulating wildly for us to hurry back.

And back we went.

Despite the fact that I had been frightened at the time and felt even more frightened as we spent what seemed an interminable time in getting the raft back to the safety of the shore, I was thrilled with the realization that we had secured photographs which might well be unique.

× XII ×

A RACE

FOR PLUNDER

While we had been busily engaged in trying to photograph whales, Murl Emery had given his attention to his beloved project of beachcombing.

Following my appraisal by plane Murl had convinced me of my mistake. He had shown me enough in an hour on the Tote Gote to make me reverse my opinion and convince me this beach was a veritable treasure-trove of interesting objects. I had found many glass balls from the Orient, a varied assortment of bottles, any number of burned-out electric light bulbs, and a lot of interesting wreckage. On our earlier exploration, Peggy had found a bottle with a note sealed in it.

This note had been badly damaged because water had seeped into the bottle, just enough moisture to cause condensation and make the note impossible to read. The note was in feminine handwriting and dated ten years earlier. It was written in Spanish, and from the occasional words we could make out and the style of handwriting, it had apparently been written by a young woman who was in desperate need of help. She had put a letter in the bottle and entrusted it to the elements.

It may be mentioned in passing that there were many bottles with notes. Some of them were notes from institutions studying ocean currents, asking the finder to mail the enclosure, together with the date and place where the bottle was found. Some of them were prank notes, obviously inspired by a sense of humor on the part of personnel in the Navy.

Emery had concluded that the part of the beach which was really worth combing was about six to nine miles north of where we were camped. He made one preliminary expedition with his Tote Gote, but didn't have enough extra gasoline along to fight his way through the deep sand after the tide came in. He was unable to get as far as he wanted to go and still stay on the safe side; but returned nevertheless with a prize assortment of loot, things which would delight the heart of a beachcomber.

What we didn't know at the time was that we were engaged in one of those peculiar "truth is stranger than fiction" coincidences.

On his first trip down to this country, Emery had conceived the idea of getting a stripped-down car over on the virgin beach. Years before Emery had been faced with the necessity of getting a car across the Colorado River. He had stripped the car down to bare essentials and then by using two boats and a lot of ingenuity had managed to get the car across the river.

So, when Emery had seen a Mexican with a pick-up that had been stripped down to wheels and engine and not much

A pickup stripped down to wheels, engine and not much else.

else, Emery had suggested loading the car on a boat and crossing Black Warrior Lagoon.

The Mexican had told Emery he was crazy, but Emery had expostulated at length on his idea, telling the Mexican just how he had ferried his car across the Colorado.

The Mexican remained firm in his opinion that Emery had polluted a naturally weak mind with too much loco weed, tequila and marijuana. In short, there was no sale.

As we were to learn subsequently, this Mexican, a man named Sande, is a very remarkable individual. Thinking back on our dealings with him, I only wish that we could make him a Secretary of State or a Minister of Finance. Our troubles would be over. We would have a balanced budget, there would be an end of the Cold War and we would be sitting pretty.

Sande is a thinker. Sande has an innate ingenuity, and if he had ever taken up chess, would have been a world champion.

Sande's mind started toying with the idea that the crazy gringo had put up to him. The more he thought about it, the more feasible the idea sounded.

So Sande looked around until he found a boat of the right size, battered and ancient enough so that it could be obtained at a moderate price. He stripped a truck down to bare essentials. A rather flat gasoline tank tilted on its side became the dashboard. A couple of light boards became the seats. There was no such thing as a hood, mudguards or body. The truck consisted of a motor, a gasoline tank, a radiator, four wheels and a frame. It was a light pick-up type which had a gear ratio permitting it to go anywhere.

So when there was a low, low tide, Sande parked his boat on the hard sands of the beach at Guerrero Negro and drove the pick-up over the boat. Then he jacked up the pick-up and removed the wheels. He lashed the pick-up firmly to the old battered boat and waited for the tide to come in to see if it would float.

The tide came in. The battered old boat did its stuff and Sande had a few inches of freeboard. He found himself in possession of a boat and a truck nicely afloat on the waters of Guerrero Negro.

So then Sande got a skiff and he and his two sons slowly, patiently and laboriously inched their strange load across the water until they came to a place where they could make a landing on the island. They tied up their craft and waited for the waters to subside as the tide went out.

Then Sande put on the wheels. Lo and behold, he had the first gasoline-powered motor ever to land on a virgin beach.

Now as it happened, within less than two hours of the time that Sande landed his strange assortment on the north end of the beach, Emery was landing his Tote Gote on the south end of the beach, with a determination to explore the beach thoroughly and see what it contained.

It is almost inconceivable that this could happen, but happen it did.

It took Sande a little while to get organized, to ferry gasoline over and set up a camp. It took Emery a little while to work out a system of carrying spare gasoline for his Tote Gote, loading a canteen of water and lunch.

At last, however, Emery's plans were complete. He started from the south end of the beach, determined to go clean to the north end.

On that same day, and within a few minutes of the same time, Sande and his two sons started their old jalopy, ran down to the firm sand on the low tide and started south with a determination to see what was on this beach the gringo had told him about two years ago.

Appropriately enough, Sande had christened his skeleton pick-up "Tírame III." (THROW ME AWAY, THE THIRD.)

Emery, going north on his Tote Gote, convinced that he had reached a section of beach where human foot had never trod, looked up and was astounded to see what appeared to be a gasoline vehicle bearing down on him from the north.

At the same moment, Sande and his two sons, convinced by this time that they were in a veritable treasure-trove of lumber and shipwrecks, with all the world to themselves, looked up and saw a strange apparition creeping toward them.

As the distance shortened and the two vehicles came together, Sande saw, to his amazement, the same bearded gringo who had first propositioned him about getting a gasoline vehicle on the beach two years ago. And Murl Emery saw, to his amazement, the fruition of the idea he had suggested to a Mexican who had at the time dismissed the whole thing as being impractical.

The two men dismounted and proceeded to exchange greetings. Each had the idea that he wanted to be the first to explore the beach, each was somewhat suspicious of the other, each determined to adapt himself to the new situation so the other didn't win *all* the advantages.

Emery advanced the proposition that, after all, he wasn't interested in lumber. He had only a light Tote Gote and couldn't carry anything. He was interested in exploring and finding what was on the beach, in taking photographs and in getting a few glass balls and other interesting souvenirs. He suggested that his time was very limited. He would only be on the beach for a few days. Sande, on the other hand, had the entire summer ahead of him and could, of course, have all the lumber—and lumber in Baja California is precious.

Emery pointed out that he had companions who were tremendously interested in exploring a virgin beach, but the Tote Gote would only carry one person. His friends had insisted that he should be selfish with the Tote Gote and explore the beach himself. But Emery knew that his companions desperately wanted to see what was on the beach.

So why not capitalize on the situation? Why shouldn't Sande turn his skeleton pick-up, the Tírame III, into a taxicab, come down to our camp, pick us all up and show us what was on the beach so that we could all see it together? This would only delay Sande's operations by one day and there would be money—much money.

Sande was cautious. How much money?

Emery tried to be equally cautious, but by that time it was too late. He had exposed his hole card.

Sande had a considerable knowledge of English which he tried to conceal behind a mask of ignorance. Emery has a fragmentary knowledge of Spanish which he tried to enhance, behind a false front of linguistic erudition.

The men sat on the beach and bargained.

At length, Sande made his final proposition. He would come to our camp at one o'clock the next afternoon. He would take us up the beach and back so that we could see it. He would charge us twenty dollars in American money. He wanted a gallon of lubricating oil and five gallons of gasoline delivered F.O.B. our camp.

Emery squirmed and twisted, but Sande was obdurate, so Emery made the bargain and returned, still somewhat dazed, to tell us that on this virgin beach which had never been trod by human foot he had hired a taxicab.

The next day we all bundled up against the rigors of a rapid transportation where there would be no windshield, no doors, no mudguards, where we would have to cling to the steel frame of a pick-up by ropes and make improvised seats out of pieces of driftwood. And we waited.

We waited and we waited and we waited. One o'clock came and went. Two o'clock came and went. And then, when there remained only two hours of daylight, Sande showed up.

Emery protested he was late.

Sande shrugged his shoulders and went into voluble Spanish. Gandara wanted to act as interpreter.

Sande didn't want any interpreter. He and Gandara clashed fire right from the start.

Sande had made a bargain. He was entitled to twenty dollars in American money, five gallons of gasoline and a gallon of oil. He wanted it.

Emery protested it was too late to do any good.

Sande was indignant. He had made a bargain. Did the gringos want to see the beach or not? There was not much daylight left.

We wanted to see the beach. We bundled up, tied pieces of driftwood on to the frame and started off.

It was a wild ride and a wonderful experience. We had to go about five miles before we came to the place where the beach really got good, and came to our first wreck.

I only wish there had been time really to study these

168

Finding our first wreck.

wrecks. Looking at them, one is surprised to find the inherent strength which has been incorporated by the builders in constructing ships. And then, as one sees the wreckage, one is equally surprised at the force of the water which tears down the work that man has done.

Here were old wrecks with oak timbers, reinforced with huge bolts, double hull construction fastened together with steel, and all twisted and battered simply by the force of water. Here were acres of glass balls, miles of intriguing flotsam. It would take many days even to explore the stuff that was there.

As we advanced farther north, however, it became apparent that the reason for Sande being late was that he had been outwitting the gringo with the Tote Gote. He had apparently put in the entire morning and most of the afternoon staking out claims to various interesting bits of wreckage. The entire north half of the beach was staked out with Sande's

169

Sande's claim.

claims and crisscrossed with tracks from the Tírame III.

Emery noted this circumstantial evidence with an increasingly dour appraisal.

The sun dipped low in the west. A cold wind began to blow in from the ocean. Sande took Emery to one side and expostulated. Emery took me to one side.

"We're late," he said.

"I know we're late."

"It's getting late. It's going to get dark."

"I know that it's late and it's going to get dark."

"Sande tells me that if he is going to show you the rest of the beach up to his camp it will be necessary for him when he returns to bring his two sons with him and spend the night at our camp."

"There isn't any room."

"They will take care of that. They will cling to the truck in some way. But that's the only way you can see the rest of

the island. Otherwise, you'll have to turn back from here, because when Sande gets to his camp he won't have time to drive back to our camp, which is a good fifteen or eighteen miles, and then return to his camp."

Sande stood aloof during all of this argument. He had the trump cards and he knew it.

So it was agreed that we would explore the north end of the island and pick up Sande's sons and they would spend the night at our camp.

We dashed on into the cold dusk, noticing everywhere that Sande had staked out claims to the most interesting and potentially profitable bits of wreckage.

We came to Sande's camp, and then it became abundantly apparent that this strategy had all been carefully worked out in advance. His sons had their bedrolls all ready and were awaiting our arrival.

There was a scene of hurried activity while the sons threw

171

their bedrolls on to the frame, put on stray pieces of driftwood, lashed the whole thing in place and we started back into the teeth of the wind.

That wind became more and more biting. The sun dipped down behind the horizon. The tide was coming in. We had to hurry. Occasionally we went through patches of soft sand where everyone had to get off and push. Then we would get down to the waterline where the wheels would be churning up water.

There was no protection by way of body or by mudguards. Sand and salt water covered my glasses. Sand and salt water covered the exposed side of my face. Sand and salt water got in my ears. Sand and salt water got down my neck. The wind cut like a knife. It got too dark to see anything. All I wanted was a campfire and warmth.

I realized that we were paying something like a dollar a mile for the experience.

The entire north half of the beach had been staked out by Sande. It was a nice gesture. However, he had apparently left the south half for Emery and his Tote Gote. As it happened, the north half was by far the most desirable, but Sande had camped on the north half and we had camped on the south half. That was the way the cookie crumbled.

So we reached our camp after dark.

The wind began to blow hard and sand began to drift from the big dunes back of camp, hitting my face so that it stung the skin.

It was a rather bleak and bitter camp.

The captain of the boat suggested to Sande that he and his two sons might want to get out of the wind and so could spend the night in the hold of the boat. The offer was accepted with alacrity.

We suffered through a windy night with fine particles of sand blowing in a veritable sandstorm and covering every-

Big sand dunes back of camp.

thing.

In the morning, Sande and his two sons emerged from the boat. They had spent a warm night away from the wind, but the boat had been bobbing around quite a bit and one of his sons had been seasick.

Sande, however, still kept his poker face. He wanted his twenty dollars. He wanted his gallon of oil. He wanted his five gallons of gasoline.

We paid Sande off and he and his two sons started back to camp in their strange vehicle.

We had breakfast and then Emery started out to the north in his Tote Gote.

Pretty soon he was back with a wry expression on his face. Sande had manipulated things in such a way that he had

Another of Sande's claim stakes.

had a good hour and a half head start up the beach. He and his two sons were engaged in putting out claim stakes on everything on the *south* half of the beach. Emery had finally caught up with them—at least to a point where he could see them in the distance. Sande and his two sons were stopping the car here and there and running—yes, running—to drive claim stakes into the beach.

Sande had staked the whole beach from north to south. He had completely outsmarted us. He had received twenty dollars and enough gasoline and oil to enable him to stay on the job and exploit his claims.

Emery gripped the stem of his pipe in his teeth, filled up a

Emery, gripping his pipe, says nothing.

can with an extra supply of gasoline, took a canteen of water and a can of beef and said nothing. There was nothing he could say—and he knew it.

He did have one trump card.

On the excursion last night he had noted a place where the beach went back for probably a mile and a half into the sand dunes in what had perhaps once been a lagoon. Emery felt certain that the Tote Gote would traverse that, and that the claim-staking Mexicans couldn't get to that section of the beach in their truck.

It turned out Emery was right.

He returned late that night with the Tote Gote literally laden with loot. He had picked up a wooden basket reinforced with woven bamboo strips which had drifted over from China and which had, in all probability, been carried for many miles on the end of a bamboo pole by some coolie transporting night soil to a rice patch. But it was now worn by waves and drifting sand, bleached clean by tropical sunlight.

Emery had, indeed, found a section of virgin beach. Deep tracks in the sand showed that the Tírame III had struggled in vain to get through the sand and had finally been forced to give up. Sande simply couldn't afford to get stuck with the only vehicle on the island, nor could he afford to waste precious gasoline in churning his way in low gear through deep sand.

Emery had found a place where there were hundreds of acres strewn with glass balls from the Orient, with bits of interesting flotsam, with glass bottles that the intense sunlight and the passing of many years had turned to a very deep purple. He had also found one glass ball which had become opalescent because of sunlight and salt encrustations. He had found a hand-carved crossbow which had drifted all the way from some tropical island. He had found a torpedo, a

176

Emery returns laden with loot.

wrecked airplane of World War I vintage, the helmet of an aviator.

Emery was a happy man, but he had been forced to leave literally thousands of glass balls which intrigued the collector in him, and would have been worth a fortune in the curio stores in the United States. He had been forced to leave dozens of bottles that had been turned, not simply to an amethyst hue one frequently finds in the desert glass, but to an absolutely deep purple by the action of the sunlight. He had encountered shipwrecks of old sailing ships which were more than a hundred years old. He had encountered all sorts of driftage, stuff that he hadn't even had time to examine. But there were no claim stakes, and, just to show that he wasn't to be trifled with, Emery had staked out a claim to the whole beach. Not that he ever expected to see it again, but it would at least let Sande know that the gringos were not entirely dumb.

I don't think Emery knows how to play chess, but he fancies himself as an expert poker player. Somehow or other, however, I have the idea that he wouldn't like to play stud poker with Sande.

× XIII ×

JUMPING AND
FEEDING WHALES

We wanted more whale photographs. Hollywood wanted me. Everyone knew that Hollywood wanted me. Hollywood was engaged in broadcasting messages on ship-to-shore wireless; and various and sundry boats, picking up those wireless messages, knew that I was encamped in Scammon's Lagoon and that Hollywood wanted me.

The script writers were going on strike and it was absolutely imperative that we have enough scripts ahead to finish the season on the Perry Mason show. And those scripts had to be stock-piled and revised before the writers went out on strike.

Moreover, we were now engaged in a battle with the wind. The wind was howling day and night. Sand was drifting from the sand dunes, covering our sleeping bags as though they had been left out in drifting snow. Sand was

Drifting sand covers everything.

covering everything, and the waters of the lagoon were rough enough so that it was very difficult to see the whales and virtually impossible to get a good photograph.

With such wind blowing it would be an uncomfortable, if not a somewhat risky, trip back to Guerrero Negro.

One afternoon the wind went down. The captain felt that it would be calm until early the next morning. So we hurried out to the boat to take more pictures. We desperately wanted a picture of a jumping whale.

These whales jump up out of the water without any preliminary warning. When they come up into the air they are moving fast. It takes a lot of momentum to propel thirty-odd tons of dead weight eighteen to twenty feet into the air.

I don't want to pose as an authority, but it is my belief

180

that a whale can only really stand on his tail during periods of absolute calm when there are no currents in the water. Under those circumstances, he can climb up out of the water, balance himself with his tail and take a good long look around.

When the water is choppy and there is a great deal of wind, when tidal currents are running swift, the whale who wants to look around leaps out of the water something like a fish. If he comes straight up, he can't seem to stand on his tail but simply shoots up perpendicularly out of the water and then is gone almost before one has had a chance to see him.

So we waited impatiently in the boat, cameras cocked waiting for a whale to jump.

I had a long focal-length lens and got some rather interesting pictures of whales jumping in the distance.

And, as subsequent events turned out, I got one picture that I didn't even know I had because I was using a long focal-length lens and looking through the finder of the camera when I shot the picture. It wasn't until after I got home and developed the picture and enlarged it that I realized I had quite a photographic prize, at least as far as I was concerned. I had a picture of a whale actually feeding in Scammon's Lagoon.

This whale was squirting many gallons of water out of his mouth, trapping the small animal life as the water was squirted through his "teeth." Something had made him come up out of the water so, as he started up, he was squirting a veritable stream of water out of each side of his mouth.

He was quite far away and through the finder I had only a brief glimpse of a whale coming up out of water, then dropping back with a splash. My eye wasn't quick enough to catch what was actually happening in the small image that was in the finder. But, as it turned out, I snapped the shutter at

Perhaps the only photograph ever taken of a
whale feeding in Scammon's Lagoon.

a five-hundredth of a second, and at the critical moment when the whale was disgorging the water and before the splash had enveloped everything.

There can be no question that this is a picture of a whale feeding.

So far as I know, it is the only picture of the sort ever taken. I have seen the pictures taken on both of the Donald Douglas-Paul Dudley White expeditions to Scammon's Lagoon. I have studied the photographs in the different books. I have never seen anything quite like this picture of the feeding whale. It may be unique.

However, back on the boat I didn't know what I had and we were waiting impatiently for a whale to jump, looking off in the distance, hoping that if one jumped within four hundred yards we could still get a fair picture.

Suddenly and without warning a whale shot up, right by the side of the boat.

We couldn't tell exactly how high he went. I thought he went about as high as the mast, but he caught us all off base. Gandara jumped to his feet and tried to point his camera. I was on the wrong side of the boat and part of the cabin was between me and the whale. I could see only a small part of him.

The whale submerged and we sat there bemoaning our fate and cursing the luck, wondering what strange hoodoo protected whales from the lens of the camera.

Jean, who had been on the lower deck, was modestly silent. She had only recently picked up photography and no one had paid much attention to her shutter clickings. At length, she modestly proclaimed, "I think I got part of him. I pointed the camera and clicked the shutter."

Still no one paid very much attention.

It wasn't until later on, after we had returned and developed Jean's pictures, that we found she indeed had a picture

Jean's picture of a jumping whale.

of a jumping whale. She hadn't been able to snap the shutter at the moment of his greatest ascendancy. He was probably about halfway up or down when her shutter clicked. But the fact remains that she had a picture of a jumping whale, and, while I didn't know it at the time, I had a picture of a feeding whale.

In any event, after it became too late in the afternoon to expect any good photographs we went ashore and started getting the camp together. The captain's prediction held true. It was virtually a windless night and the morning was calm.

With the first streaks of daylight we were rolling things down the beach and aboard the boat, and shortly after sunup we were on our way.

Three hours later we were unloading stuff on the wharf at Guerrero Negro and considerate hosts at the salt works suggested that the girls and I leave the work of unloading and reloading in the trucks to the others while I went to headquarters to telephone and answer telegrams which had been piling up.

The more I saw of those telegrams the more I felt it would be better not to engage in a lengthy conversation over the ship-to-shore wireless. And, in any event, it was a Saturday afternoon.

It turned out that Mr. McClaughry had to go to San Diego the next day and the executive plane was coming down to pick him up. He very kindly offered to take me in with him, knowing that it is almost impossible to get a charter plane over the weekend in Baja California. Nearly all of the planes are engaged in regular scheduled runs over the weekend, taking sportsmen down to the various resorts that are springing up.

We were anxious to get to the Bahia de Los Angeles because we had been hearing so much about it. We wanted to see it and it was agreed that the rest of the party would

185

start out that afternoon and camp along the road. I would wait overnight and fly into San Diego with McClaughry.

So the others started out, I waited over and shortly after noon Sunday, found myself in San Diego, renting a car from the Hertz Company, and I blessed the forethought which had caused me to take my special Hertz credit card along. My appearance was so disreputable that if it hadn't been for that credit card I might have had some trouble even convincing the Hertz people that I could be trusted with a car.

So once again I had a hectic period ahead of me. I drove to the ranch, got busy on the long-distance telephone, told everyone where I was and started work.

Thanks to my battery-powered dictating machine, I already had quite a bit of material dictated and was able to leave those discs for the girls to transcribe on Monday. (Only two of my secretaries are free to travel. The others have "committed matrimony," live within driving distance of the ranch and come in during the day.)

Scripts had been arriving by mail, and after I telephoned, a messenger was hurriedly dispatched from Hollywood with still more scripts. I telephoned Francisco Munoz and asked him if he would be free to take me to the Bahia de Los Angeles where I could join the others on Tuesday morning.

Munoz was very regretful. He was all tied up for Tuesday. He was tied up for Monday afternoon. But Monday morning, early, he could take me.

I had a good two days' work stacked up, but somehow I did it all in one night.

Early Monday morning I jumped into the rented car and took off for San Diego.

Never have I seen such a fog!

Driving through that fog was a harrowing experience, particularly as I was late in getting started. I wouldn't care to repeat that ride. But somehow I reached San Diego and got there on time. Munoz was waiting impatiently. I asked him about the field being socked in at Tijuana.

He gave me a smile and a characteristic shrug. "It is clear on the other side," he said.

That settled it.

We got down to Tijuana. The field was socked in. Aircraft which should have taken off for Mexico City at six o'clock were still sitting there. The airport was thronged with stalled passengers.

Munoz took it all in his stride. He hurried around getting things ready, and while he was doing it, the fog began to lift a bit here and there. Munoz is a professional optimist, and his optimism always pays off.

Munoz helped me into the plane, we fastened the seat belts and were off. By this time there was a certain amount of visibility, but if there hadn't been I feel certain I would have been in Bahia de Los Angeles right on schedule just the same.

Francisco Munoz is a careful pilot, but he is one of the old school of lobster pilots who made a living by putting planes down on the beaches at lonely lobster camps, picking up lobsters and flying them back to market. The men who engaged in that work were like the postman—rain, hail, sleet and fog were impediments but never any reason for delay. The lobsters had to be flown. And these men are great pilots.

We broke out of the fog at around two thousand feet and from there on the trip was beautiful. I always love to fly over the peninsula of Baja California and look down on the roads I have traversed so laboriously. Moreover, on this trip we flew directly over the Sierra San Pedro Martir, a district which I had always wanted to see.

I had heard much about this country, a wonderful mountain plateau on which there is pine timber and lush grass, where there is running water, trout in abundance and any

Bahia de Los Angeles.

quantity of deer.

We were flying at around eleven thousand feet and when we came over the mountain plateau we seemed to be within less than fifteen hundred feet of the plateau.

It was a beautiful trip; and then we were over the mountains and out on the Gulf side and I was looking down on the road we had so recently traversed with our automobiles.

A very short time later I was leaving the plane at the resort of Antero Diaz on the Bahia de Los Angeles. I found that my caravan had arrived only a matter of minutes earlier.

We settled down to living deluxe.

We had rooms. There was running water. The water was not hot except during the middle of the day when the sun would heat five-gallon coal oil cans on the roofs sufficiently to make the water pleasantly warm. We were sleeping in beds, out of the wind and away from the drifting sands.

And we were eating. Holy suffering mackerel, *how* we were eating!

I have eaten in many of the best restaurants in the world. I have arrived at an age when I try desperately to count the calories. I have never had grub such as that at Casa Diaz on Bahia de Los Angeles, and I threw the calorie chart out of the window.

Breakfasts are rather conventional: eggs, bacon, hot cakes.

Lunch, however, is really something. It is a big meal. All of the meals are big.

A typical lunch may include meat from the huge turtles which are indigenous to the Gulf, a juicy tender meat with a distinctive flavor; frijoles that are cooked as only a Mexican can cook frijoles, wonderful, thin, chewy tortillas and a little fried fish on the side.

The rock of the circular window.

There is always fish available.

Fillets of freshly caught fish stacked like cordwood.

There is always fish available.

There are enough fishermen going out in boats to keep the larder and the town, and probably the whole peninsula, well stocked with fish.

Whenever a boat comes back, the truck automatically goes down to load the fish. They are brought up literally by the truckload. A skilled Mexican with a sharp knife spreads the fish out on a cement slab and cuts fillets from the sides, avoiding all bones, avoiding all fins and getting only the strip of fine, firm meat between the skin and the backbone.

These fillets are stacked up on the side of the trough like cord wood.

People who live around the resort and who want fish simply come and take them. It is a common sight to see a couple of five-year-olds struggling to get their prize home—a fish that will weigh fifteen to twenty-five pounds, which has been freshly caught and is hard to handle.

The fish in those waters represent just about the best eating in the world and the cooks are very, very expert at preparing them. They have been doing it all their lives and that fish, fresh out of the water, is a treat for the palate which simply can't be described.

Or perhaps a meal may consist of abalone and chicken, or some equally interesting combination.

There is always all you want to eat and more in the kitchen.

Clams, oysters? . . . Sure, help yourself.

A man can go out into the clam beds and dig enough clams with his fingers to get a wonderful clam cocktail. Or he can go over to the bed of rock oysters and, with the aid of a stout knife, have absolutely fresh oysters on the half shell.

And then there are the lobsters.

The lobsters usually come with the evening meal; huge platters of lobsters cut in half and drenched in drawn butter.

Clams for the digging.

Those lobsters have a wonderful flavor. They are fresh, well-cooked and the meat is sweet and tender. You don't want to feel like a hog and therefore try to hide the shells so that your neigbors can't see how many you're eating.

Antero Diaz understands that feeling perfectly and he is a considerate host. He will glide unobtrusively behind your seat and pick up the empty lobster shells and remove them so that you can tackle more lobsters with a clear conscience.

There is a rumor that lobsters cause nightmares.

If lobsters really cause nightmares I can assure you I will have nightmares for the next five years. I have eaten enough of the lobsters at the Bahia de Los Angeles to guarantee my quota of nightmares for that time.

However, the food there doesn't cause nightmares, it doesn't cause indigestion. It does give one a drugged, sleepy, relaxed feeling and, except on weekends when the sportsmen

Gathering rock oysters.

come thronging in by airplanes, it is seldom one hears human voices after nine o'clock at night.

The cost?

Your room and three meals a day will cost you such a small amount you feel you are robbing the guy.

There were interesting people at the Bahia de Los Angeles—

O. W. ("Tim") Timberman and his wife, Pat.

Timberman was an oil executive in Tucson. Came the inevitable day when the nerve strain levied its toll. He had always wanted to travel and explore, and his wife had wanted to paint.

So Timberman walked off the job, bought a small truck, put a home on wheels, and started for Baja California.

Since that time, he has explored the length and breadth of the peninsula. He knows and loves the people and the people know and love him. His wife has developed a remarkable skill with her paint brush and the two drift up and down the peninsula, familiar with all the roads, visiting with people who know them and love them. They have the reputation of being "muy simpatico."

When the Timbermans start along the road the word goes ahead by that mysterious grapevine telegraph which seems to function perfectly in a land where there is little traffic and where one would think news could never travel.

Timberman has written a book entitled, "Mexico's Diamond in the Rough" which is the latest book on Baja California and which contains bits of interesting information which can be found in no other book. It is a book which should be read as it was written, in the quiet relaxation of philosophic leisure. It is a book which tells of roads and adventures, of families and of interesting personalities. It gives little traits of the Mexican character and, not only in the lines but in between the lines, is the picture of two people who

194

Seals fishing in Bahia de Los Angeles.

have found happiness and contentment after having spent much of their lives in the competitive rat race of a highly keyed-up existence.

Any person who is approaching the age of retirement and wonders just what he is going to do should read Timberman's book, should read of their wanderings up and down the peninsula; of the table which is supplied quite largely by their own efforts and the generosity of their friends: white-winged doves, fish fresh out of the ocean, lobsters, clams, oysters, roast of venison, and other delicacies.

There were other interesting people at the Bahia de Los Angeles: Faye B. Howard and her companion, Mrs. Nina Hartmann.

Mrs. Howard is by way of being one of the greatest living experts on shells. She is, however, inordinately modest. To hear her story one would think she was nothing but a refugee grandmother, a fugitive from being engulfed into an existence of perpetual baby-sitting.

Faye B. Howard, one of the greatest living
authorities on shells.

Actually she is not only an outstanding authority on sea shells but has had several species named after her. She has made startling discoveries in the field, and as a result of these discoveries some scientific theories have to be completely overhauled. She has, for instance, discovered shells which had heretofore been found only in fossils and which were supposed to belong to a long past era, not only in the form of non-fossils but actually occupied by the living mollusk.

She and her companion also have one of these houses on wheels; a little home which can be put on the bed of a pick-up and which furnishes protection from the weather, enough room for eating and sleeping; a sort of laboratory; and yet does not have enough weight or bulk to interfere with driving, even over pretty rough roads.

There was one drawback at the Bahia de Los Angeles. We were a little too close to civilization.

Here was a ship-to-shore telephone where we could call people and where people could call us. Here was a regular pattern of airplane transportation. While we were two and a half or three days from the border by four-wheeled-drive vehicle, we were only two and a half hours from Tijuana by air.

We had some films which I wanted developed and I didn't want to let them out of our possession. I wanted Sam to develop them personally. I was also afraid that I had kept Sam away from his home so long that his family might not recognize him on his return. So I suggested Sam fly back with Francisco Munoz, develop his films, and return a couple of days later.

Gandara found that the Governor of Baja California was very much interested in an exhibit of Baja California which was to be staged at a fair in Los Angeles. We had some very interesting material which could go into that booth, so Gandara hopped a plane for Mexicali and Los Angeles.

Munoz delivered Sam, then flew back to Bahia de Los Angeles with some passengers. He had about twenty-four hours at his disposal so I suggested Murl Emery, Jean and I make the trip to Loreto by air.

A suggestion of this sort to Munoz is instantly acted on. Why wait?

Why, indeed?

The words were hardly out of my mouth before we were hurriedly loading cameras and light overnight bags. We fastened the seat belts and were off.

Flying over Baja California is a most interesting experience. It is always fascinating to look down on ground which is virtually untrod by human foot.

Science has uncovered evidence indicating that up to about three hundred years ago Baja California was blessed with a very considerable amount of rainfall. Then within the last three hundred years the creeping cycle of drouth began to make itself manifest. A country that at one time supported many thousands of Indians now has become parched for lack of water. And valleys which must at one time have teemed with human life and abounded with game now are lying deserted in sun-drenched silence.

What would a person find in the way of relics and artifacts if he could get into some of these valleys?

Some of them still remain fairly well watered. From the plane one can see tall palm trees growing in profusion, casting cooling shade. One can see a trickle of water. But there is just about no way anyone could get into those isolated garden spots. There are no roads within miles and miles and miles. One couldn't transport enough water to enable a burro to get there. And so, one can look down on canyons which are probably filled with metallic riches; on dry valleys and mesas which at one time supported much life; on intriguing canyons and natural oases where there is water, food and shade; but there is absolutely no practical method of finding out exactly what is there. It is a virgin country. However, the use of four-wheel drive vehicles is making quite a difference and the influx of tourist dollars is making a difference. Roads are going to be constructed and it won't be too long before adventuresome individuals who want to explore country which has never been touched in modern times can find that country within a few hundred miles of San Diego.

It is an interesting thought.

"Tim" Timberman had suggested that by all means we should go to a point some twenty miles south of Loreto on the Gulf, where we could see the Shangri-La where he and his wife had spent many happy weeks; a gulf within a gulf, completely surrounded by protecting hills, with an opening only a few yards wide leading to the waters of the Gulf itself. Timberman told me it was about six miles around the shore line, and from the air it looked to be all of that. It is a paradise for the hunter and fisherman and the deep, tranquil blue of the water lying serene, protected from winds from any direction, a shoreline ringed with sandy beaches alternating with deep water along sheer mountains, offers limitless opportunities for leisurely existence and quiet exploration.

Timberman told me that once I had seen it I would never be happy until I managed to get there, and I am afraid he is right.

Loreto, one of the first cities of Baja California, was just beginning to recover from the devastating effects of a terrific *chubasco* (the Baja California version of the tropical hurricane).

There had been winds up to well over a hundred and twenty miles an hour. Rain had descended in torrents, had spread down from the hills in a flood. Adobe bricks had dissolved like sugar lumps in hot coffee. Palm trees had been

199

School children and teacher, Guillermo Yee F., at Loreto.

toppled like broken toothpicks, and many lives had been lost.

Here and there rubble and wreckage was slowly being cleared away; but the town, with indomitable spirit, was carrying on. In the course of its long existence it had survived flood and earthquake and the people were philosophical. They had taken refuge in the old mission, and the handiwork of the ancient priests had again justified their faith. The stone structure had remained immobile while trees were crashing and buildings were collapsing.

New construction was springing up from piles of rubble, and I was impressed with the schoolhouse. Despite the surrounding wreckage of disaster the schoolhouse was new, modern and the pupils were bright and alert. No matter what else had to be done, the school had priority.

As we walked past, school was just letting out and one of the teachers was marching the pupils around for a period of exercise. I came along with a camera and started snapping pictures. Then, after the class was dismissed, I shook hands with the teacher and became acquainted. He was of Chinese-Mexican descent, and had that wonderful patience which I have found so frequently in the Mexican school teacher.

There is something about the Mexican school discipline which inspires obedience and respect, yet which leaves the individual free to manifest and develop his own individuality. It is as though teacher and pupil were in partnership.

My arrival with a camera quite naturally interfered with the drill, if it could be called such, but both teacher and pupils took that in their stride. The pupils had a desire to co-operate and the teacher knew they had that desire. They were also curious about the photographer and about the camera.

I have never heard a harsh word in a Mexican school house. I have never seen a pupil who seemed insubordinate. I have seen many who made faces, who smiled, who took liberties, but I have never seen one who was insubordinate or insolent and I have never seen a nervous Mexican school teacher.

It is in comparatively recent years that Mexico has learned to emphasize the importance of education, and within the next few years we are going to see some remarkable results.

Also in Loreto I found an enthusiastic reader fan, a tomato grower named Al Green, who took me into his house to show me a big supply of Gardner books translated into Spanish.

He had at one time read *The Land of Shorter Shadows* which had been loaned to him by a friend and was very anxious to get a copy of that book—however, as previously mentioned, it is a book which is now out of print and which has become a collector's item.

Jean had two treasured copies of the book and, before we left, Green's enthusiasm was such that she had agreed to send him one of her two copies.

When we departed Green was on hand with plenty of ripe tomatoes neatly packed in cartons so that we would

Senor Al Green, the tomato king of Loreto, and his wife show the author a case of luscious tomatoes ready to be shipped by air.

have enough tomatoes to last us on our trip to the border —big, luscious, ripe tomatoes and, as we later found out, sweet and flavorful.

Many parts of the United States were being gripped in blizzards at the moment but Al Green was shipping tomatoes to California and had been shipping them all winter.

It was quite an operation. He and members of his family had ranches where they grew the tomatoes. They were brought in to a packing house, sorted and packed, then shipped by airplane to the United States. The operation was expensive but the tomatoes commanded a premium because they were so well grown and well selected, and Al Green told me that the Safeway Stores took his entire output, willingly paying the premium in order to get such choice tomatoes on their shelves.

It was hard to tear ourselves away from his enthusiastic hospitality, but we were really traveling on a tight schedule and we were somewhat concerned because the fog had now descended on the Gulf side, and Loreto had low visibility and, wonder of wonders, a drizzling rain.

But Munoz took all this casually and we were off on schedule and soon out of the clouds and into the bright sunlight.

We returned to the Bahia de Los Angeles and then Munoz promptly took off for Tijuana to bring Sam back the next day.

I should of course have known what was going to happen when Sam came back. Fortunately, I didn't.

Leo Roripaugh, a neighbor of mine in Temecula, an adventurous sportsman and a skillful aviator, was vacationing at Bahia de Los Angeles—a place he had learned to know and love—and we sat through a leisurely evening in the warm, velvety darkness watching the stars reflected in the water and talking about how nice it was to be completely relaxed, and free from the evils of too much nerve strain.

The next day Munoz was late in arriving and we were

Francisco Munoz, skillful aviator takes everything in his stride.

somewhat worried but about four o'clock he came in and touched down on the landing strip with that deft skill which comes with years of flying. He taxied up to the place and Sam emerged from the plane with a whole file of important messages: There were more scripts in Hollywood; the strike had been moved up; I must get back *at once*.

My publisher had two books awaiting proofreading; The Detective Book Club was in a hurry for one written under the pen name of A. A. Fair, and a Perry Mason book was scheduled for immediate printing. There were stacks and stacks of important mail—vital matters which needed immediate attention.

I tried to charter a plane to get back, but to no avail. Munoz had a full load for the next day. It was now getting late. All of the charter planes were filled up on the weekend.

So we dashed into our rooms and hurriedly threw things helter-skelter into the automobiles. We had only an hour before darkness but an hour was an hour.

We hastily shook hands and were off, engulfed once more in the exigencies of civilization.

Baja California is a land of serene charm. There are rugged places in the road. It is a land which is still largely unexplored. There are ghost cities and abandoned mines. There are places like Las Flores out of the Bahia de Los Angeles where ambition and capital started a great mining town and imported machinery and even a railroad engine, cars and track.

These things were all brought in by water. Then they were landed and laboriously taken apart so that they could be transported by human power and on the backs of burros. Then they were reassembled. A city sprang up some seventy years ago. For a while there was great prosperity and buildings were erected. The town even needed a jail, and that jail, constructed of stone, not only still stands, but etched in the stone one can find places where the repentants scratched a tally of the time they had served as each day of their sentence became a yesterday.

There were graveyards; one graveyard for the rich on the west side of the town; another graveyard for the *peon* on the east.

Now the distinction between rich and poor has been obliterated by the passing of time. It is as hard to find one graveyard as the other. We did find one grave with an iron marker still in place, grown over with desert plants.

We found old machinery and dilapidated wreckage. We found the remnants of an old civilization, but the once teeming city was now wrapped in the dignity of death; the mysterious, quiescent period which is as much a part of life as birth itself.

There are quite a few such ghost cities in Baja California. There are the ruins of old missions which were established by the padres when they sought to convert the teeming population of Indians. There is adventure in Baja California, and

Ghost cities and abandoned mines.

there is something even more rare. There is serene tranquility; and there can always be found the touch of human humor.

When we were returning from our first trip, as we approached the border we stopped at one of the "swanky" restaurants which are beginning to appear here and there.

This was a magnificent establishment, with subdued lighting, the soft strains of gentle hi-fi music, waiters resplendent in white shirts, dinner jackets and colored bow ties. The menu had an impressive array of items covering the gamut of sea foods, wild game and various cuts of steak.

We were tired and hungry. We had had a long, hard day and we wanted something good to eat.

I took a look at the menu and suggested to Gandara that he speak to the headwaiter and find out what was the best dish which we could get without too much delay. I rather suspected that with such a wide variety on the menu some of the dishes were more staple and in instant readiness.

So Joe called over the headwaiter and there began one of the most spirited conversations in high-speed Spanish I have ever listened to. Words were rattling like hail on a tin roof. The conversation developed into an animated argument.

After it had gone on back and forth for some two or three minutes, Jean caught my attention. "Look here," she said, "I don't want Joe ordering for *me*. I want to pick out what *I* want. It's all right for him to find out what is best in the kitchen but I want to do my own ordering."

Joe heard her, nodded his head and motioned with his hand that she wasn't to worry, everything was well, and then plunged once more into rapid-fire conversation with the headwaiter.

The headwaiter gestured emphatically with his hands. Joe raised his eyebrows in incredulity. He barked staccato questions and the headwaiter answered volubly.

It was late and I was afraid the dining room would close

before the conservation terminated, so I kept nudging Joe to speed it up.

Joe would nod over his shoulder, so to speak, and then resume the verbal barrage.

Finally it got down to a point where it was apparent there was a meeting of the minds. Joe's questions became shorter and while the note of incredulity still remained in his voice it was apparent that he was getting at the gist of the thing.

The headwaiter became more and more emphatic but his statements were shorter.

It was apparent that he and Joe had established a basis of friendship and the headwaiter was answering Joe with complete candor—a candor which was, perhaps, too complete.

Finally Joe sighed and turned to us and picked up the menu.

"Well, Joe," I asked, "what did he say?"

Joe said, "He told me, '*Here, I would order nothing except beans.*'"

With one accord we looked at the long menu and burst into uproarious laughter.

The headwaiter, who understood very little English, looked at us with a puzzled expression. There was no accounting for the vagaries of American tourists.

Once the land of Baja California has stamped its charm upon you, you can't remain away very long at a time. Those who have known this peninsula continue to love it and to return to it—and those who have hunted whales in Scammon's Lagoon are marked men. Whale hunting is too exciting not to leave an indelible mark. Next January I have an idea we will be back in Scammon's Lagoon, and I wouldn't be too surprised if next year didn't find Donald Douglas back among the whales.

Too few people know anything about Baja California. The roads in places are bad. The climate is wonderful. The marine scenery is unsurpassed, and there are literally thousands of potential resort sites within a short distance of the heavily populated centers of Southern California.

As my friend, Donald Douglas, pointed out in a recent conversation with me, the technical and scientific developments in the field of converting sea water into good drinking water are destined to have a terrific impact on the future of Baja California.

In the vicinity of Los Angeles there are hundreds of thousands of sportsman who are fed up with the fished-out streams they so frequently encounter, who would give their eye teeth to drop a line in virtually virgin waters, well populated with hungry fish. Yet within one or two hours flying time of Los Angeles there are these blue waters, literally filled with fish. There are white sand beaches, a relatively gentle, curling surf, a climate which combines the dryness of the desert with the cool, moist breezes blowing off the ocean.

It seems inevitable that Baja California is on the threshold of a great expansion.

I know some of the prominent people who are in business in Baja California. They are interested in promoting better international relations and in making the country more accessible to the tourist. As air transportation becomes faster, safer and more economical, more sportsmen are going to become familiar with this country, and as tourist traffic justifies it, roads are going to be built and improved and resorts are going to spring up.

Baja California is a land of adventure, and more and more people are going to become familiar with the charm of a country where dry air, warm sunshine, cooling breezes and blue waters present an irresistible combination for sports and recreation.